Joseph E. Stiglitz, a Nobel laureate in economics, is university professor at Columbia University and chief economist at the Roosevelt Institute. He is the author of *The Stiglitz Report*, a co-author of *Mismeasuring Our Lives*, and a co-editor of *For Good Measure* (all published by The New Press).

Jean-Paul Fitoussi is professor emeritus at the Institut d'Etudes Politiques de Paris (SciencesPo), Paris, and professor at LUISS Guido Carli University, Rome. He is a co-author of *Mismeasuring Our Lives* and a co-editor of *For Good Measure*.

Martine Durand is the chief statistician and director of statistics of the OECD. She is a co-editor of *For Good Measure*.

MEASURING WHAT COUNTS

MEASURING WHAT COUNTS

THE GLOBAL MOVEMENT FOR WELL-BEING

JOSEPH E. STIGLITZ,
JEAN-PAUL FITOUSSI,
AND MARTINE DURAND

THE
NEW
PRESS

NEW YORK
LONDON

The use of this work, whether digital or print, is governed by the Terms and Conditions to be found at http://www.oecd.org/termsandconditions. Requests for permission to reproduce selections from the Introduction should be made through The New Press website: https://thenewpress.com/contact.

A version of this book was first published as Stiglitz, J., J. Fitoussi, and M. Durand (2018), *Beyond GDP: Measuring What Counts for Economic and Social Performance*, OECD Publishing, Paris, https://doi.org/10.1787/9789264307292-en.

Published in the United States by The New Press, New York, 2019
Distributed by Two Rivers Distribution

The opinions expressed and arguments employed herein do not necessarily reflect the official views of OECD member countries.

This document, as well as any data and any map included herein, are without prejudice to the status of or sovereignty over any territory, to the delimitation of international frontiers and boundaries and to the name of any territory, city or area.

The statistical data for Israel are supplied by and under the responsibility of the relevant Israeli authorities. The use of such data by the OECD is without prejudice to the status of the Golan Heights, East Jerusalem and Israeli settlements in the West Bank under the terms of international law.

ISBN 978-1-62097-569-5 (pb)
ISBN 978-1-62097-570-1 (ebook)
CIP data is available

The New Press publishes books that promote and enrich public discussion and understanding of the issues vital to our democracy and to a more equitable world. These books are made possible by the enthusiasm of our readers; the support of a committed group of donors, large and small; the collaboration of our many partners in the independent media and the not-for-profit sector; booksellers, who often hand-sell New Press books; librarians; and above all by our authors.

www.thenewpress.com

Book design and composition by Bookbright Media
This book was set in Adobe Garamond and Avenir

Printed in the United States of America

10 9 8 7 6 5 4 3 2 1

This report is dedicated to the memory of Alan B. Krueger.

Alan played a central role in the Commission on the Measurement of Economic Performance and Social Progress and in the High-Level Expert Group, especially through his work on subjective well-being and the ways it links to other life domains.

Brilliant academic, dedicated public servant, valued colleague, and dear friend, he helped transform the understanding of labor markets, showing (with David Card) that an increase in minimum wage does not have the adverse employment effects previously claimed. He brought his deep economic insights, combined with his strong focus on data, into the realm of policy when he served as Chairman of President Obama's Council of Economic Advisers, where he advocated for policies that promote equality and opportunity.

Alan understood the power of economics to transform our society— to reduce human suffering and to improve societal well-being. He dedicated his life to these lofty goals.

We will sorely miss him. He was more than a brilliant mind; he was above all a good person who sincerely cared for people.

CONTENTS

MEASURING WHAT COUNTS

INTRODUCTION

The world is facing three existential crises: a climate crisis, an inequality crisis, and a crisis in democracy. Will we be able to prosper within our planetary boundaries? Can a modern economy deliver shared prosperity? And can democracies thrive if our economies fail to deliver shared prosperity? These are critical questions, yet the accepted ways by which we measure economic performance give absolutely no hint that we might be facing a problem. The standard measure of economic performance is gross domestic product (GDP), which is the sum of the value of goods and services produced within a country over a given period. GDP had been humming along nicely, rising year after year, until the 2008 global financial crisis hit. According to the GDP metric, since then the US has been growing slightly more slowly than in earlier years, but it's nothing to worry about. Any concerns voiced or studies published about a slowdown in productivity or growth have been largely ignored. Politicians suggest slight reforms to the economic system and, they promise, all will be well. In Europe, the impact of 2008 was more severe, especially in countries most affected by the euro crisis. But even there, apart from the highly elevated unemployment numbers, standard metrics do not fully reflect the magnitude of the suffering and the adverse impacts of the austerity measures.

It is clear that something is fundamentally wrong with the way we assess economic performance and social progress. Even worse, our metrics too frequently give the misleading impression that there is a trade-off between the two; that, for instance, changes that enhance people's economic security, whether through improved pensions or a better welfare state, come at the expense of national economic performance.

Getting the measure right—or at least a lot more precise—is crucially important, especially in our metrics- and performance-oriented society, where we judge ourselves by how well we do in certain well-defined measures. If we measure the wrong thing, we will do the wrong thing. If our measures tell us everything is fine when it really isn't, we won't make the right decisions. And it should be clear that, in spite of the increases in GDP, in spite of the 2008 crisis being well behind us, everything is *not* fine. We see this in the political discontent rippling through so many advanced countries, and we see it in the widespread support of demagogues, whose successes depend on exploiting economic discontent.

My own interest in these topics goes back a long time. When I was a graduate student in the 1960s at MIT, I realized that economics (as it was then) had given short shrift to information, including to the imperfections of information and to the costs of gathering, processing, and disseminating information. Thus began a major strand of my future research: the development of the economics of information, for which I received the Nobel Memorial Prize in 2001. Accounting systems, as imperfect as they might be, are the way we organize information. We have corporate accounting systems, tracking the performance of companies, and we have national accounting systems, tracking the performance of national economies. But these accounting systems don't always give us the information we need.

After I entered government as a member and then chairman of the Council of Economic Advisers under President Clinton, I grew increasingly concerned about how we measured economic performance. There were many flaws, but the one that absorbed my attention was the failure to measure environmental degradation and resource depletion. If our economy seemed to be growing but that growth was not sustainable because we were destroying the environment and using up scarce natural resources, our statistics should warn us. But because GDP didn't take resource depletion and environmental degradation into account, the measure was giving us an excessively rosy picture of how well we were doing. Working with the Department of Commerce (the federal agency that calculates GDP), the Council of Economic Advisers proposed that there should be a new measure, now often referred to as a *green GDP*, to take into account environmental degradation and resource depletion. We knew we were on to something important when we were met with strong opposition from the senators and representatives of the coal states. They threatened to cut our funding if we continued our work. They realized the importance of *metrics*, of how we measure things. It is but a short step from assessing and measuring the costs imposed on our society by coal mining and coal burning to doing something about these costs, including taxing and regulating. If one showed that the coal industry might actually be reducing *correctly measured* GDP, then reining in the coal industry might be viewed as a good thing because it would increase GDP.

In 2008, France's then-President Nicolas Sarkozy asked Jean-Paul Fitoussi, a distinguished economist at Paris's Institut d'Études Politiques de Paris, known as SciencesPo,[1] Nobel Prize winner Amartya Sen, and me to chair an international Commission on the Measurement of Economic Performance and Social Progress, to reassess the adequacy of current metrics and to suggest alternative approaches. The question was clearly topical. We easily managed to assemble a distinguished and diverse international group of social scientists (including several who were already or were about to become Nobel Prize winners). We identified crucial weaknesses with metrics and suggested remedies, but, most importantly, we argued that economists and governments could not capture anything as complex as our society in a single number. We needed a dashboard if we wanted to reflect the many dimensions of success or deprivation—including inequality, economic insecurity, and sustainability. We also argued that the very process of coming to an understanding of the aspects of our economy and society that deserved attention would itself strengthen democratic processes—something that many thought was a central dimension of a well-performing society.

As we note in the pages that follow, we were more than pleased with the international reception of our report, which helped create and sustain a global movement, one that centered on redirecting societal efforts at enhancing the well-being of individuals and communities and promoting new ways to assess progress in achieving these broader societal objectives. And this movement—bringing together social and environmental scientists, statisticians, and civil society—has now succeeded in introducing these ideas into policymaking in a few vanguard countries like Scotland, Iceland, and New Zealand. This was, of course, our ultimate objective: to change governmental policy-making in ways that would enhance societal well-being. We are optimistic that these trends, so evident today and described in greater detail in Chapter 4 below, will be strengthened in the years to come.

The timing of our report in 2009 couldn't have been more opportune in some ways, but in other ways was unfortunate. The global financial crisis itself illustrated deficiencies in commonly used metrics, because they had neither given policy-makers nor markets adequate warning that something was amiss. Though a few astute economists had sounded the alarm, the robust health indicated by the standard metrics seemed to suggest everything was fine. A major message of this report is that, subsequently, inadequate metrics provided poor guidance in how to respond, resulting in (or at least contributing to) policy decisions that have left deep scars in many places, especially in Europe, that may take years to heal.

But the timing was inopportune in that with so much focus on the Great Recession and then on the euro crisis, there was little appetite among officialdom for the continuation of our technical work in improving the system of metrics. Recovery was the priority. But in the meantime, not only did the movement we described earlier flourish, the OECD, and especially the office of the Chief Statistician, took up the cause, in 2011 launching a new biennial report, *How's Life? Measuring Well-Being*, and creating the Better Life Index, an interactive tool that provides data on a wide variety of measures that make for a "good life," allowing users to compare countries' performances in ways that reflect people's own values.

In 2013 a High-Level Expert Group (HLEG) was formed and housed at the OECD to continue the work started by the Commission. (In practice, there is little difference between an "expert group" and a Commission.) The OECD provided enormous institutional and intellectual support, without constraining in any way the Commission's work, and for that we are very grateful. As we describe more fully below, the group was chaired by Martine Durand, chief statistician of the OECD, Jean-Paul Fitoussi, and me.

We made three critical decisions in shaping the direction of our work: (1) that we would focus particularly on policy-making—designing statistical frameworks that would be of particular relevance for policy-makers, and devoting efforts to thinking about how these metrics would help shape policy; (2) that we would expand our membership to include heads of some of the key national statistical offices around the world in order to increase the chance that our ideas would be both implementable and implemented; and (3) that rather than attempt to write a consensus report, we would disseminate our results in two forms, a chair's summary (this volume) and authored chapters, presenting research results in some of the key areas discussed by the HLEG.

We should emphasize the key role of the group as a whole. This volume represents our summary of the deliberations of the group, which itself chose and shaped the topics to be discussed. There was, in fact, remarkable consensus among members on most of the issues though, inevitably, different members put more emphasis on one point or another. We chose this particular approach, not uncommon in commissions with a diverse membership, because reaching an agreement on wordsmithing would have diverted attention away from our main objective, which was to advance work in developing better metrics of economic performance and social progress. (The group as a whole also played a key role in shaping the papers in the accompanying volume of authored chapters, entitled *For Good Measure: An Agenda for Moving Beyond GDP.*[2] Each of the topics was discussed extensively by the HLEG, often with a special meeting devoted to the issues, typically with contributions also made by researchers who were not members of the HLEG.)

We decided to focus the group's attention on two broad themes. The first, a direct follow-up of the earlier Commission on the Measurement of Economic Performance and Social Progress, was to trace the evolution of the *beyond GDP* movement and its impact in the aftermath of the report. We wanted to assess, too, how changes in the world in the years after the report would affect—and perhaps reinforce—the relevance of the report and its impact. (These topics are discussed particularly in Chapters 1 and 4.)

As it turned out, the following decade was an eventful one: the world agreed on a set of Sustainable Development Goals—a set of norms governing what society should strive for; the climate crisis worsened faster than had been expected. The world also agreed on objectives to cope with the degradation of the environment at the 2015 United Nations Climate Change Conference in Paris. Inequality reached new heights. And the Great Recession morphed into the euro crisis. Each of these changes reinforced our earlier claim that we needed better tools to assess economic performance and social progress. Fortunately, a variety of advances in both methodology and technology have provided us with those better tools. Most importantly, there have been significant improvements in our ability to collate data from different sources, including administrative data (such as tax records) and surveys.

Secondly, the Commission itself had as one of its central objectives laying out an agenda for future work: the fewer than two years the Commission had for deliberations were simply too short to do anything else. There were many topics we felt were of primary importance, and we hoped that drawing attention to them would inspire others to work in these areas. Much of the HLEG's time was spent focused on these topics, and the chapters in the accompanying volume represent the efforts of those who spearheaded the HLEG's investigation into each of the areas. Not surprisingly, we focused on bringing into our accounting frameworks concerns about inequality (both horizontal and vertical, both of income and of wealth, and of opportunity), economic insecurity, volatility, sustainability, subjective well-being, and trust. The list itself suggests just how deficient GDP is in assessing social progress. To accomplish its goal, the HLEG organized itself into four working groups: Theme I—Income and Wealth Inequality; Theme II—Multidimensional and Global Inequalities; Theme III—Multidimensional Subjective Well-Being; and Theme IV—Sustainability.

What we have accomplished so far has convinced us of two things: First, that it is possible to construct much better measures of an economy's health. Governments can and should go well beyond GDP. And second, that there is far more research to be done. In Chapter 5, we lay out some of the next steps in the agenda.

In the months since completing our report and its initial distribution, we have been pleased both with its reception and the continued strengthening of the global *beyond GDP* movement.

We launched the report in 2018 in Incheon, Korea, at the 6th OECD World Forum on Statistics, Knowledge, and Policy, whose theme was "The Future of Well-Being." More than 2,700 people from 104 countries attended. Much of the discussion was about the report's specific areas of focus. A consortium of countries, called Wellbeing Economy Governments (WEGo), has had its initial meetings, and New Zealand has introduced well-being metrics into its budgeting processes. Bills have been introduced in the US Congress to have the kinds of distributional national accounts that we discuss in Chapter 3, and other countries are also constructing such accounts.

I want to add my personal thanks to the members of the High-Level Expert Group for their hard work and deep intellectual contributions, which should be evident in the following pages; and to those who made the work of the HLEG possible (listed in the Preface below). To these, I need to add a few more: to Andrea Gurwitt, Debarati Ghosh, Sarah Thomas, and Caleb Oldham, who helped manage my own contributions to this effort; and to Marc Favreau and Emily Albarillo of The New Press. The New Press's publication of the Commission's report under the title *Mismeasuring Our Lives: Why GDP Doesn't Add Up* played an important role in disseminating the ideas of the Commission,[3] as did the two French volumes published by Odile Jacob: *Richesse des nations et bien-être des individus* and *Vers de nouveaux systèmes de mesure.* I am confident that the publication of this and the companion volume will play a similarly important role in spreading the work of the High-Level Expert Group on the Measurement of Economic Performance and Social Progress.

Joseph E. Stiglitz

PREFACE

This short book provides our personal perspective, as Chairs of the Organisation for Economic Co-operation and Development–hosted High-Level Expert Group on the Measurement of Economic Performance and Social Progress (HLEG), on the most salient issues discussed by the Group over the past five years (from 2013 to 2018). Over this period, the HLEG periodically convened to discuss many of the issues that are reflected in this book. The HLEG, whose members are listed on pages 215–16, was created to pursue the work of the Commission on the Measurement of Economic Performance and Social Progress convened by former French President Nicolas Sarkozy in 2008 (the "Stiglitz-Sen-Fitoussi Commission"). A companion volume, *For Good Measure: An Agenda for Moving Beyond GDP*, provides a series of authored chapters, prepared by some HLEG members, on those topics that have been the focus of the HLEG work, and which are also discussed here.

While this book presents our own perspective on the deliberations of the HLEG, it rests on the enormous contributions of its members—not just the authored chapters in the companion report but also the extensive discussions and deliberations, both in our plenary meetings and in the thematic workshops. Full credit needs to be given to the HLEG members for their huge intellectual contributions, which are reshaping how we think about the measurement of economic performance and social progress.

Any group of this kind, dealing with complex and important issues, faces an insoluble dilemma. To get agreement among all HLEG members on all the salient issues is extraordinarily difficult and time-consuming. As we undertook this new phase of the work, with greater constraints and higher ambitions, the Group decided to have authored chapters on each of the topics upon which it would focus—with the hope that each of these chapters would take into account the deliberations and comments of other HLEG members.

At the same time, we believed it important to provide an overview of the issues that we discussed. The Group therefore agreed that there would be a Chairs' summary, reflecting and taking into account the views of all members of the HLEG. It was understood that not every member would agree with each of our interpretations of the issues. Some members might not even agree that we have captured accurately the spirit of our deliberations, though, based on the feedback we have received from members, we are confident that we have been able to strike a good balance.

We feel remiss that we have not been able to give individual credit to each of the ideas that each HLEG member has contributed. They have been selfless in their dedication to this project, and we are deeply grateful. All we can say is "thank you."

Our thanks also go to the OECD, for having hosted the work of the HLEG during this five-year period, to the many foundations and organizations who hosted and financially supported the organization of the thematic workshops, and to the many researchers who attended these workshops and shared with us their expertise on these subjects. These workshops have focused on:

- "Intra-generational and Inter-generational Sustainability" (September 22–23, 2014), Rome, hosted by the Einaudi Institute for Economics and Finance and the Bank of Italy and sponsored by SAS;
- "Multi-dimensional Subjective Well-Being" (October 30–31, 2014), Turin, Italy, organized in collaboration

with the International Herbert A. Simon Society and Collegio Carlo Alberto, and with the support of Compagnia di San Paolo;

- "Inequality of Opportunity" (January 14, 2015), Paris, hosted by the Gulbenkian Foundation in collaboration with Sciences-Po Paris and the CEPREMAP;
- "Measuring Inequalities of Income and Wealth" (September 15–16, 2015), Berlin, organized in collaboration with Bertelsmann Stiftung;
- "Measurement of Well-Being and Development in Africa" (November 12–14, 2015), Durban, South Africa, organized in collaboration with the Government of South Africa, the Japanese International Cooperation Agency, Columbia University, and Cornell University;
- "Measuring Economic, Social and Environmental Resilience" (November 25–26, 2015), Rome, hosted by the Einaudi Institute for Economics and Finance, supported by the Bank of Italy and ISTAT, and sponsored by SAS;
- "Economic Insecurity: Forging an Agenda for Measurement and Analysis" (March 4, 2016), New York, organized in collaboration with the Washington Center for Equitable Growth, the Yale Institution for Social and Policy Studies, and the Ford Foundation; and
- "Measuring Trust and Social Capital" (June 10, 2016), Paris, organized in collaboration with Science-Po Paris and the European Research Council.

We would like to express our special thanks to a number of colleagues who have supported our work throughout this period: Marco Mira d'Ercole, for his many valuable inputs to this book; Elizabeth Beasley, for acting as rapporteur of the authored volume; Martine

Zaïda, for coordinating the HLEG and organizing all the thematic workshops and plenary meetings; Patrick Love, for his inputs and for editing the books; Christine Le Thi, for statistical assistance; and Anne-Lise Faron, for preparing these books for publication.

FOREWORD

The release of the Report by the Commission on the Measurement of Economic Performance and Progress in September 2009 was a defining moment. During his presentation of the Report, the then President of France Nicolas Sarkozy said: "In today's circumstances, this report is important not just technically (but) also politically. It deals with questions that concern not only economists, statisticians and accountants, but also politics, and as a consequence, the whole world." The Report's key message was simple: change the focus of our statistics from measuring the size of economic production, which is what GDP is about, to measuring what shapes the well-being of people today and that of future generations. This change of perspective is crucial, in the words of Nobel laureate Joseph E. Stiglitz—one of the Commission's Chairs: "What you measure affects what you do."

This message resonated well with the OECD, where statistics are at the core of our evidence-based policy advice, and where, as early as 2004, we had been advocating for the expansion of our measurement frameworks to capture not only aggregate economic performance, but also people's quality of life. So we were well placed to follow up on President Sarkozy's call that the OECD should play a critical role in implementing the Commission's recommendations at the international level. In 2011, we adopted our new motto "Better Policies for Better Lives," and we launched the OECD Better Life Initiative, which has played a key role in advancing the "Beyond GDP" agenda, through our flagship publication *How's Life?* and the OECD Better Life Index.

Our contribution has not been limited to measures and statistics though. In 2012, in the aftermath of the devastating global financial crisis, we launched the New Approaches to Economic Challenges (NAEC) Initiative, an organization-wide reflection on why we did not see the warning signs, and in what ways we could change our "GPS" (our data, our models, and our tools) in order to establish the basis of a better way for analyzing economic challenges and improving our policy advice. Moreover, in the same year, we launched our Inclusive Growth project, aimed at jointly analyzing "growth" and "inequality," which had, until then, been looked at separately, sometimes leading to inconsistent policy recommendations. Building on this work, this year we launched the OECD Framework for Policy Action on Inclusive Growth, which aims to guide policy-makers in designing policies that distribute the benefits of growth more equally, and to give people a fair chance to achieve their full potential. While we may not have traveled the full distance, we are now better equipped to address today's realities and challenges. For these reasons, I very much supported the suggestion of our Chief Statistician, Martine Durand, that the OECD was the ideal place to "host" an independent group of experts, convened by Joseph E. Stiglitz and Jean-Paul Fitoussi, to maintain the momentum of the 2009 Commission and provide further direction to the "Beyond GDP" agenda.

This book provides an overview by the Chairs of the OECD-hosted High-Level Expert Group on the Measurement of Economic Performance and Social Progress (HLEG), summarizing almost five years of work. I would like to thank Joseph E. Stiglitz, Jean-Paul Fitoussi, and Martine Durand for their leadership, and all HLEG members for their dedication and contributions.

I very much hope that the views expressed in this book, and in the companion volume, *For Good Measure: An Agenda for Moving Beyond GDP*—which are offered in the authors' personal capacity—will have the same significant influence in the economic and statistical community as that of the 2009 Stiglitz-Sen-Fitoussi Commission. It is only by having better metrics that truly reflect people's lives and aspirations that we will be able to design and implement "better policies for better lives."

Angel Gurría
OECD Secretary-General

OVERVIEW

The High-Level Expert Group on the Measurement of Economic Performance and Social Progress (HLEG) builds on the analyses and recommendations of the 2009 Commission on the Measurement of Economic Performance and Social Progress (the Stiglitz-Sen-Fitoussi Commission) in highlighting the role of well-being metrics in policy and encouraging a more active dialogue between economic theory and statistical practice. The report makes explicit the often-implicit assumptions hidden in statistical practices and their real-world consequences. Its central message is that what we measure affects what we do. If we measure the wrong thing, we will do the wrong thing. If we don't measure something, it becomes neglected, as if the problem didn't exist.

There is no simple way of representing every aspect of well-being in a single number in the way GDP describes market economic output. This has led to GDP being used as a proxy for both economic welfare (i.e., people's command over commodities), and general welfare (which also depends on people's attributes and non-market activities). GDP was not designed for this task. We need to move "beyond GDP" when assessing a country's health, and complement GDP with a broader dashboard of indicators that would reflect the distribution of well-being in society and its sustainability across its social, economic, and environmental dimensions. The challenge is to make the dashboard small enough to be easily comprehensible, but large enough to summarize what we care about the most.

The 2008 crisis and its aftermath illustrate why a change in perspective is needed. The GDP loss that followed the crisis was not the temporary one-off event predicted by conventional macro-economic models. Its effects have lasted over time, suggesting that the crisis caused the permanent loss of significant amounts of capital—not just machines and structures, but also "hidden capital," in the form of lower on-the-job training, permanents scars on youths entering the labor market during a recession, and lower trust in an economic system "rigged" to benefit a few.

Different metrics, including better measures of people's economic insecurity, could have shown that the consequences of the recession were much deeper than GDP statistics indicated, and governments might have responded more strongly to mitigate the negative impacts of the crisis. If, on the basis of GDP, the economy is perceived to be well on the road to recovery, as many governments believed in 2010, one would not take the strong policy measures needed to support people's living conditions suggested by metrics that inform on whether most of the population still feels in recession. Nor would one take measures to bolster the safety net and social protection in the absence of metrics on the extent of people's economic insecurity.

These failings in the policy responses to the crisis were compounded by overly focusing on the consequences of public spending in raising government's liabilities, when this spending could take the form of investment increasing the assets in governments' and countries' balance sheets. The same follows when measures of unemployment do not reflect the full extent of a country's "unused" labor resources. The "Beyond GDP" agenda is sometimes characterized as "anti-growth," but this is not the case: the use of a dashboard of indicators reflecting what we value as a society would have led, most likely, to stronger GDP growth than that actually achieved by most countries after 2008.

This book also looks at progress in implementing the recommendations of the Stiglitz-Sen-Fitoussi Commission since 2009, identifying areas that require increased focus by statistical agencies, researchers, and policy-makers. The UN Sustainable Development Goals, agreed by the international community in 2015, clearly go far "beyond GDP," but their 169 policy targets and more than 200 indicators for "global monitoring" are too many to guide policies. Countries will have to identify their priorities within the broader UN agenda, and upgrade their statistical capacities which, even in developed countries, are insufficient to monitor whether the agreed-upon commitments are being met. The international community should invest in upgrading the statistical capacity of developing countries, especially in areas where country data are needed to assess global phenomena, such as climate change or the world distribution of income.

Inequality in income and wealth has today a central role in policy discussions in ways it did not in 2009. But important progress is still needed in a range of areas, such as measuring what happens at both ends of the income distribution, integrating different data sources, and measuring the joint distribution of income, consumption, and wealth at the individual level. When looking at inequality, it is also important to look at differences between groups ("horizontal inequalities"), at inequalities within households, and the way resources are shared and managed, which are especially important in the case of wealth. We should also look beyond inequality in outcomes to inequality of opportunity. Inequality of opportunity is even more unacceptable than inequality of outcomes, but the operational distinction between the two is fuzzy, as we don't observe all circumstances that shape people's outcomes and are independent of their efforts. It is also important to pursue efforts to integrate information on economic inequalities within national accounts, to provide metrics of how GDP growth is shared in as timely a fashion as output statistics.

This book also highlights metrics that still lack a solid foundation within official statistics. Subjective well-being measures are critical to assess the nonmonetary costs and benefits of public programs and policies. While much progress has been achieved since 2009 in embedding these measures in large-sample official surveys, such efforts should be maintained to shed light on the many measurement and research issues that are still open. Economic insecurity is a "new" field where much more effort is needed to develop metrics of the shocks affecting people, and of the buffers available to them. The 2008 crisis reduced not just people's economic security but also their trust, because of the widespread perception of the unfairness in the manner in which the crisis was handled. The loss of trust (both in others and in institutions) is a long-lasting legacy of the crisis, whose effects are contributing to the political upheavals we are witnessing around the world. Finally, the measurement of sustainability in its environmental, economic, and social dimensions, and of the resilience of systems to shocks, are priorities for research and statistical practice, requiring the contributions of different disciplines and approaches.

The book provides 12 recommendations for further work in all these areas, which complement those in the Stiglitz, Sen, and Fitoussi (2009) report.

While different measures are clearly needed, alone they are not enough. What also matters is to anchor these indicators in the policy process, in ways that survive the vagaries of electoral cycles. This book draws on country-experiences to show how well-being indicators are being used in the different stages in the policy cycle, from identifying priorities for action, to assessing the advantages and disadvantages of different strategies to achieve a given policy goal; help allocate the resources needed to implement the selected strategy; monitor interventions in real time as they are implemented; and audit the results achieved by policies and programs to help decide how to change them in the future. Steps taken by several countries in this direction are described in this book. While these experiences are recent, they hold the promise of delivering policies that, by going beyond traditional silos, are more effective in achieving their goals and that could help in restoring people's trust that public policies can deliver what we all care about: an equitable and sustainable society.

1.

The Continued Importance of the "Beyond GDP" Agenda

This chapter looks at what has changed since the 2009 Commission on the Measurement of Economic Performance and Social Progress (Stiglitz-Sen-Fitoussi Commission). It describes the contribution of the High-Level Expert Group on the Measurement of Economic Performance and Social Progress (HLEG) to moving "beyond GDP" when assessing a country's health, toward a broader dashboard of indicators that would reflect concerns such as the distribution of well-being and sustainability in all of its dimensions. The challenge is to make the dashboard small enough to be easily comprehensible, but large enough to include a summary of what we care about the most. The chapter argues that what governments measure strongly influences what they do. If they do not regularly include income inequality or economic insecurity in their dashboard of indicators, for example, they may not notice that these are getting worse. The chapter also argues that distorted metrics can lead to misleading assessments—for example, gauging success solely through the lens of GDP while failing to measure the potential environmental damages caused by economic activities.

Introduction

In January 2008, before the global financial crisis, President Sarkozy of France established a Commission to examine the adequacy of our metrics for assessing economic performance and social progress. He, like many others before him, was worried that too much attention was placed on GDP as an overarching measure of performance. GDP, as we all know, is a measure of the volume of goods and services produced within a country over a given period of time. It is not—as it is often used—a measure of a country's success.

This is not a new complaint. Just over 50 years ago, Robert Kennedy gave expression to similar concerns:

> Gross National Product counts air pollution and cigarette advertising, and ambulances to clear our highways of carnage. It counts special locks for our doors and the jails for the people who break them. It counts the destruction of the redwood and the loss of our natural wonder in chaotic sprawl. It counts napalm and . . . nuclear warheads and armored cars for the police to fight the riots in our cities. It counts Whitman's rifle and Speck's knife, and the television programs which glorify violence in order to sell toys to our children. Yet the gross national product does not allow for the health of our children, the quality of their education or the joy of their play. It does not include the beauty of our poetry or the strength of our marriages, the intelligence of our public debate or the integrity of our public officials. It measures neither our wit nor our courage, neither our wisdom nor our learning, neither our compassion nor our devotion to our country, it measures everything in short, except that which makes life worthwhile. (Kennedy, 1968)[1]

In spite of its shortcoming as a measure of a country's success, GDP has remained its key proxy. We take measures like GDP for granted—until they fail us. Much of this book is about the discovery of how this metric has failed us when used for purposes that it was not designed to address, and about what can and is being done to create measures that better reflect changes in economic performance and social progress.

It was not until after the Great Depression that governments started to collect the data necessary to measure GDP. Keynesian economics—which explained the level of economic output in terms of the demand from different sectors of the economy and argued that government action could maintain the economy at full employment—made it imperative to have better indicators in order to assess the state of the economy.[2] Two economists, Simon Kuznets, of the University of Pennsylvania, and Richard Stone, of Cambridge University, received Nobel Prizes, in part for their contribution in setting up the System of National Accounts (often abbreviated as SNA), which includes GDP, a concept developed by Kuznets.

For a while, economics students had to learn the ins and outs of these metrics, the assumptions that went into them (and why those assumptions were made), and the limitations of these measures and their uses. GDP and other national accounts indicators became part of the tool kit of economists. Careers were built trying to explain the movements of GDP and to show how these movements could help explain that of other indicators. This trend was reinforced by economists' growing ability to analyze data statistically, as a result of better computers.

But, as time went by, and as the sophistication of analyzing the inter-relationship among different data series increased, the attention paid to the data series themselves, and in particular, to the limitations of GDP as a welfare metric, declined. The result was that the reliability and relevance of results of analysis in areas, such as macro-economics, that were heavily reliant on GDP measures may have declined too. The paradox is that those who built the system *knew* of its shortcomings and were cautious when using it.[3] But as the general understanding of these indicators and their construction diminished, their use became more widespread and their limits were forgotten by most users. While GDP had been designed and used to measure market activity, increasingly it became a thermometer used for assessing the general health of societies.

Simon Kuznets warned against this risk more than 50 years ago:

> As a general formula, the desirability of as high and sustained a growth rate as is compatible with the costs that society is willing to bear is valid; but when using it to judge economic problems and policies, distinctions must be kept in mind between quantity and quality of growth, between its costs and returns, and between the short and long run. . . . Given the variety of qualitative content in the overall quantitative rate of economic growth, objectives should be explicit: goals for more "growth" should specify more growth of what and for what. (Kuznets, 1962)[4]

The issues discussed in this book may, at first sight, appear to be technical, and addressed to a narrow field of specialists. But they are not only technical: they go to the root of how our democratic systems function. In the words of President Sarkozy, the goal of the Commission was to address

> A gulf of incomprehension between the expert certain in his knowledge and the citizen whose experience of life is

completely out of sync with the story told by the data . . .
nothing is more destructive of democracy. . . . People
believe that they are being lied to . . . that they are being
manipulated." (Stiglitz, Sen, and Fitoussi, 2009)[5]

This gap between the "experts" and the citizen they are supposed
to be serving has played an important role in the bitter divisions
within society that have been so vividly demonstrated in a number
of recent elections. President Sarkozy was thus prescient in drawing attention to the consequences in a democracy of a growing gulf
between the statements, assertions, and beliefs of the experts and
elites, on one side, and the lived experiences of significant numbers
of citizens, on the other.

The Commission had as one of its central missions ensuring
that our metrics drew our attention to those things that made a
difference to people's lives. One thrust of this book is that, had
the recommendations of the Commission been more fully
implemented—and some of the issues developed in this volume
more fully explored—different policies might have been chosen.
There were early warning signs not only of the discontent, but also
of the underlying changes in our economy and society that might
have been expected to give rise to such discontent. Whether that is
so or not, one thing is clear: metrics matter, and in both the financial crisis of 2008 and what some have called the political crisis of
2016, our SNA, centering on GDP, did not give us adequate warning of what was around the corner. Some may say that was not the
purpose, that was not what national accounts were designed to do.
But surely it would have been good for society to have *some well-
established and widely used* indicators of the major traumas that were
about to befall.

GDP Statistics and the Great Recession

Even when focusing on market income, national accounts statistics may sometimes fail to provide the full picture. In September 2008, the United States—and then the world—fell into what has been called the Great Recession, the worst global downturn since the Great Depression 80 years earlier. As the economy was about to slip into recession, leading economists pronounced the economy to be in good health.[6] A few years earlier, the longtime head of the US Federal Reserve, Alan Greenspan, dismissed worries about the possibility of a bubble in asset prices by saying that there was just a little "froth."[7] These leading economists had taken the vital signs of the economy and pronounced it fit and healthy.

In retrospect, there were a number of failures. Those in positions of power, who have to decide whether, for instance, to tighten or loosen credit if they judge the economy to be, or about to be, over- or under-heated, rely on a variety of indicators—just as medical doctors take a patient's pulse, monitor blood pressure, take a blood cell count, look at whether the patient is gaining or losing weight, and so on. Indicators that could have provided a warning signal to policy-makers of what was about to happen were, in many cases, available but were not part of a well-established reporting system and were mostly ignored by those who should have noticed. In other cases, these indicators were simply not available—e.g., sectoral accounts and balance sheets that led (post-crisis) to several initiatives aimed at improving the kind of information available to decision makers.[8] In yet other cases, early estimates of GDP failed to provide a sense of the true scale of the recession, and were heavily revised in later periods.[9]

Most fundamentally, policy-makers ignored these warning signals because of the ideological blinders that prevented them (and their economic advisers) from seeing the dangers ahead. They were also reassured by conventional macro-economic models that said that a crisis of such proportions could not happen. They took comfort from past movements in GDP, in the hope that the "Great Moderation" (combining good GDP performance with lack of inflationary pressures) that prevailed before the crisis could extend into the future.

A year later, as GDP began to increase in 2009, President Obama announced that the economy was on the mend, that recovery in the United States had begun. Yet, to the overwhelming majority of Americans, this did not seem to be the case. Again, aggregate economic indicators, such as GDP, seemed out of sync with "the facts on the ground." What was going on, what was being experienced by most Americans and by most people in the developed world, was not conveyed by the figure that is usually relied upon, GDP.

There were, of course, some simple explanations for this conundrum. One factor was that GDP growth often disproportionally benefited those at the top of the income scale: in the United States, 91% of all the gains in income in the first three years of recovery (2009–12) is estimated to have gone to the top 1% (Saez, 2016). Thus, in the United States, *most* households were not experiencing a recovery. There was a similar phenomenon in Europe, more visible in countries most affected by the crisis. In those same three years of supposed recovery, growth in *average household income* in Europe, as measured in the national accounts, lagged GDP growth,[10] while growth in *median household income*—where 50% of the population is above that level and 50% below—as measured in surveys, lagged average income growth (which was boosted by gains going to a relatively small number of people). No wonder, then, that most people felt that there was no real recovery.

A second factor was that many households lost their home and jobs, and often their hope in the future, in addition to their income. And those who didn't were fearful of doing so.

Income itself does not provide a full summary of the economic anxieties facing individuals.

One clear lesson from the crisis is the need for a broader range of statistics, including more granular data that capture the diverse situations of different groups of the population. GDP, for example, is not constructed to measure the economic situation of individual households. Indeed, if GDP goes up by, say, 5%, it doesn't mean that everyone sees their income go up by 5%, nor even that the typical household or person sees his or her income go up by that amount. GDP describes what is happening to total economic *production* and to the average income generated from this production—whether this income accrues to a few people or many, to residents or foreigners, to households or to firms. Even if the income is going to residents, GDP doesn't say how this income is distributed among households.

But the US President should have been aware (or been made aware by his economic advisers) that GDP could go up even though the vast majority of people saw no increase in their incomes—if inequality increases enough. And that was precisely what happened in the US "recovery." The single number, GDP, didn't adequately summarize what most people were experiencing. So, too, when Ireland's GDP went up 26% in 2015: it wasn't that the Irish citizens, who had been suffering so much from the euro crisis, suddenly found their worries at an end. Indeed, Irish household disposable income per capita rose by only 2.7% in that year. In this case, the surge in GDP reflected, to a large extent, the transfer of the intellectual property assets of a few multinationals to independent entities in Ireland, which much of the profits generated by these entities transferred abroad rather than benefiting Irish households.[11]

That GDP didn't do all that was hoped of it shouldn't be a surprise: no single number can summarize anything as complex as the economy. Further, an average is just an abstract number for the individuals who are averaged. But there are real consequences of relying on an incomplete set of measures. If the economy is perceived to be well on the road to recovery, according to GDP, one might not take the strong policy measures needed to resuscitate the economy that one would take on the basis of metrics that inform on whether most of the population still feels in recession. Nor would one take measures to bolster the safety net and social protection in the absence of metrics on the extent of people's economic insecurity.

If the measures we rely on are out of sync with how citizens experience their lives, a lack of trust in government will develop. Some would argue this is what happened in the United States and in most other industrialized countries in recent years, when the GDP statistics said the economy was in recovery and yet most people felt otherwise. While other factors might have been at work (Pew Research Center, 2017), the disparity between what was happening on the ground and the announced "recovery" almost surely contributed to the growing lack of trust in governments by so many citizens over this period. Most OECD countries are today facing a "trust crisis," a crisis that in some cases goes back in time. To give one example, in 2017 fewer than 20% of Americans trusted their federal government to do what is right most of the time, as compared with close to 80% of Americans in 1964 (Figure 1.1). Data for a broader range of countries show that confidence in national governments, which hovers today around 40% on average across OECD countries, fell by 10 points or more in many of the countries most significantly hit by the crisis (e.g., Greece, Spain, and Portugal) while strongly improving in countries that were less affected, such as Germany (OECD, 2017b).[12]

Figure 1.1. People's Trust in the United States Federal Government

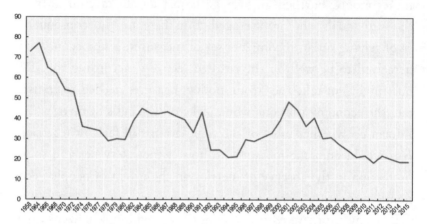

Note: Before 1985, data were not collected on an annual basis.
Source: Pew Research Center (2015), Historical trends of public trust, www.people-press .org/2015/11/23/1-trust-in-government-1958-2015. StatLink http://dx.doi.org/10.1787 /888933842014.

It was concerns like these that motivated President Sarkozy to establish the Commission. As an elected official, he worried that making claims about how well the economy was doing that did not correspond to what voters were feeling would undermine trust in the government. He worried too about the conflicting signals he was receiving as a public official. He knew that his performance would be graded partly on how well the economy did. But he also knew that voters cared about many things other than GDP—they cared about the quality of their jobs, their housing conditions, the lower opportunities of their children; they cared about pollution, noise, and other things that *ought* to have been incorporated in our measures of economic performance and social progress but were not.[13]

The Commission and Its Central Recommendations

The Commission, headed by Joseph E. Stiglitz, Amartya Sen, and Jean-Paul Fitoussi, consisted of leading economists and other social scientists.[14] Their central question was to assess GDP as a measure of performance, to identify its limitations, and to consider how better metrics of well-being and social progress might be constructed. Their recommendations were aimed particularly at statistical agencies and governments, focusing on the need for more data and research. The Commission provided a number of technical suggestions for improvements in our metrics. But at the core of its recommendations was the belief that *our measures matter,* and that we should move away from over-reliance on GDP when assessing a country's health, toward a broader dashboard of indicators that would reflect concerns such as the distribution of well-being and sustainability in all of its dimensions.

How large could a dashboard be? As citizens and officials, there are limits to the amount of information that we can absorb and process. The Commission recommended that there should be a relatively small number of indicators, with some of them reflecting how well ordinary citizens were doing (for example, measures of households *median* income may be a better indicator of the economic well-being of the "typical" person than average income, which can be pulled up by a few people having enormously high incomes) and other indicators measuring sustainability. Economic sustainability is typically captured best by some monetary measure of wealth, but environmental sustainability may be better assessed by using some physical metrics. So too does it make sense to reflect how well society was doing in terms of health by considering physical metrics of longevity and morbidity—and not even trying to convert them into some dollar equivalent.

The challenge was to make the dashboard small enough to be easily comprehensible, but large enough to include a summary of what we care about the most.

Measurement Matters

We live in a world of metrics, where we are constantly quantifying our progress, our success. What we measure affects what we do. If we measure the wrong thing, we will do the wrong thing. If we don't measure something, it becomes neglected, as if the problem didn't exist. If we don't measure inequality or environmental degradation, we are less likely to attend to these concerns.

Of course, measures will always be imperfect. That's not the issue. The real question is, Are they misleading us? And of course, even if measures are imperfect, we can't do without them. One can't imagine flying a plane without a dashboard of instruments; similarly, we can't imagine steering an economy without a dashboard of indicators. In a sense, the simple message from the Commission was that we needed a dashboard, that we must understand better each of the dials on that dashboard, and that we need to develop new dials for important problems that are still inadequately measured. To achieve all of this, we need to re-activate a dialogue in society about the final destination of our plane and the greatest risks it faces while heading there.

An Array of Problems

As important as metrics are, all metrics are beset by problems. The choice of metrics is part of the debate in many other areas of public and private life. For example, one of the responses to concerns that our schools are not doing what they should be doing is that we need better student assessments. We can then know when we are failing our children. But, putting aside the question of how those assessments are used, the question is, What should be assessed? Standard tests often focus on basic skills, such as reading, writing, and arithmetic. However, schooling is about more than that. It teaches social skills—how to get along with others. It teaches basic life skills—to show up on time every morning, to obey orders, to work as a member of a team. And it teaches higher-order cognitive skills that may foster creativity. If student testing focuses only on basic skills, teachers will focus on those at the expense of other skills. Overall, schools will perform less well—though they will perform better in the basic skills. Such considerations led to the changes introduced in the well-known OECD Programme for International Student Assessment (PISA) tests. While PISA started in the late 1990s by measuring 15-year-old students' basic skills in reading, science, and numeracy, it now also assesses "soft" skills and students' well-being in school.

A Monetary Metric

If there were a simple way of converting every aspect of well-being into a monetary figure, we could simply estimate the total money value of well-being. Together with an indication of how this value is distributed, this would provide a clear guide for increasing societal well-being: wherever possible, substitute a higher money–metric activity for a lower one. If we had the right information, we might even have a way of incentivizing people to do the right thing. In this grand conception, our money metric would reflect not just the market prices of the goods or services produced, but also the intrinsic (social) value of the activity. For example, making shoes that strengthened muscle power (the value of which was not reflected in the market price) would be valued more than one that led to muscle deterioration.

The market economy does something that is almost as spectacular. So long as all firms are small and numerous, and so too are households, and so long as there is no market failure (the exact meaning of which will be elaborated on below) and no externalities, the economy is efficient and maximizes the market value of goods and services produced.[15] Thus, if the market value of the goods and services produced increases, aggregate social well-being increases, or so it would seem.

But things are not so simple. One reason is that an economy at different moments in time has different *relative* prices and different *money* prices. The problem of higher money prices (in, say, dollars or euros) is easy to fix. That's called inflation. When we want to assess changes in the *real* output, we want to take out the effect of inflation. If, on average, the prices of all goods and services have increased by 3%, we simply reduce the change of nominal GDP by 3%, to get a measure of the change in real GDP. If real GDP has gone up, so has aggregate economic welfare. We have thus created a money metric of aggregate economic welfare.

Matters are more difficult when there is a change in relative prices, i.e., the price of one good relative to that of another. Economists and statisticians have devised ways of making approximate, but fairly good, estimates of what has happened to real GDP when relative prices change. Typically, prices don't change very quickly, and so if we assess GDP at annual intervals, the differences in most relative prices will be quite small. We can calculate the value of GDP at time $t + 1$ by using prices at time t. If that value has gone up by, say, 3%, we can say economic welfare has gone up (in our money metric) by a corresponding amount. We compare GDP in 2018 with that in 2007 by performing this exercise every year. The result is called the chain-weighted GDP index.

Beyond Mere Technical Problems

More fundamental problems arise as soon as we depart from the simple model.

For a start, much activity occurs outside the marketplace. Individuals may be given education and health care by the government, and economic production also occurs at home. Market production, on its side, does not always increase people's economic well-being, as firms may deceive their clients about the value of the goods and services that they sell.

More fundamentally, individuals' well-being is affected by factors other than economic production and the income generated by it. It is shaped by their sense of security and their relationship with others, including their employer. The simple economic model also assumes that individuals can "sell" as much labor as they want at the going wage, so that the wage measures the marginal value of leisure (or of time). This, in turn, implies that there is no unemployment, or at least that all unemployment is voluntary—i.e., individuals are indifferent (at the margin) to more leisure or to more work at the going wage—an obviously false assumption.

Further, at any point in time, there are many market failures (failures of markets to produce the fully efficient outcomes associated with the "ideal" textbook competitive market economy with full information) and all lead to market prices that differ from those corresponding to the "intrinsic *marginal* value" (the value of adding an extra unit) of goods, services, and assets that are exchanged. The existence of market failures, externalities, and public goods all implies that an economy that maximizes the market value of goods and services would not necessarily maximize aggregate social welfare, and that market prices do not adequately reflect either social costs or benefits. These market failures arise from imperfect information, market power, environmental externalities, absence of markets for important risks, public goods, deficiencies in corporate governance and bankruptcy frameworks, and a host of other problems. These market failures are pervasive; they represent not a small glitch in economic design but an inherent consequence of, say, the fact that information and knowledge are costly to produce and transmit, or that markets are costly to create and to transact on, or that it is efficient to have certain goods publicly provided or publicly produced. While in some cases the consequences may be small, in many cases they are of first-order importance, not only for ascertaining the efficiency of the economy but also for assessing the adequacy of our standard statistical measures in providing an assessment of the performance of the economy.

When we assess the conditions of the economy as a whole, there are other considerations still: most importantly, the sustainability of the economy. The present generation can be living off inherited riches, leaving nothing to the future. More broadly, societal well-being is about economic, social, and environmental sustainability, none of which is well reflected in GDP.

Finally, as a society, we care about the distribution of well-being. People may prefer patterns of economic growth whose benefits are widely shared to those where benefits are limited to a few or are concentrated among the better off.

There are thus multiple reasons why GDP is not a good measure of societal welfare.

As Kuznets warned, GDP was constructed with a much more modest ambition—measuring the level of market activity. It grew out of the Great Depression to answer a very important question: How could we quantify the loss in economic output that was evidently occurring? Over time, it has expanded into a measure of welfare: of economic welfare first, and of general welfare second. This expansion of the use of GDP is where the problem lies.[16]

The Commission on the Measurement of Economic Performance and Social Progress, and its successor, the High-Level Expert Group on the Measurement of Economic Performance and Social Progress, had as their mission the development of better metrics of economic performance and social progress, improved understanding of the limitations of commonly used metrics like GDP, and enhanced understanding of how these better metrics can lead to better policies.

The Commission looked at long-standing problems, such as the measurement of public services (where individual choices do not reveal information about individual valuations), as well as three areas: the assessment of economic inequalities, sustainability, and quality of life. The latter included the new field of subjective well-being, i.e., metrics derived from surveys administered to individuals in which respondents reflect on their life as a whole or report on their daily experiences. Such surveys have been shown to provide relevant and reliable information about individuals' well-being that is not contained in other metrics, calling attention to aspects of well-being that might otherwise be neglected: the importance of social connections, political voice, or quality jobs. For example, we know today that the loss of a job is important for more than just the loss of income that is associated with it, so that even making up for the lost income won't really restore the individual's well-being.

Later chapters of this book will look more closely at inequality and sustainability. Here, we simply reiterate their importance: what matters is not just the size of the pie, but how it is divided, the set of ingredients used when preparing it, and whether these ingredients will continue to be available in the future. An economy whose benefits are not widely shared and where whole industries, occupations, and regions are left to suffer carries within it the germs of its rejection by those who are called to adjust to conditions that are not of their making (Kuznets, 1962). Similarly, an economy whose growth is not sustainable in all its dimensions (economic, social, environmental) is stealing from future generations. It is clear, in retrospect, that GDP growth in much of the developed world prior to 2008 was not sustainable. Similarly, it should be clear today that our economic growth is not environmentally sustainable: climate change represents an existential threat. Some elements of our dashboard should have called this to our attention.

A National Dialogue

The Commission report argued that a national dialogue determining what should be included in the dashboard of indicators, and whether existing metrics properly reflected what society cares about, is an important part of democratic engagement. Since then, many civil society groups have come forward, urging changes in our measurement system, and many governments have responded through measurement initiatives (see Annex) and by taking steps to anchor well-being indicators in the policy process (see Chapter 4). The response has, in many ways, exceeded what the Commission had anticipated, reflecting growing concerns around the world over issues like income inequality and the environment. The growing participation in the OECD World Fora on "Statistics, Knowledge and Policy,"[17] which started in 2004—before the Great Recession and the establishment of the Commission—and continue to be organized periodically by the OECD to promote the "Beyond GDP" agenda, are a testimony to this success.

There is some tension, though, between the desire to have metrics that reflect the particular situation within a country and the need to have metrics that enable cross-country comparisons, i.e., to give a picture of how a country is doing relative to others. Both perspectives are important: we all want to know how well we are doing (in one dimension or another) relative to our past or relative to what is occurring elsewhere. The OECD Better Life Initiative—launched in 2011 in response to the Commission's recommendations[18] and detailed in its biennial report, *How's Life? Measuring Well-Being* (OECD, 2017a; see Annex)—provides a dashboard of well-being indicators that can be compared across OECD member countries. Individual countries have developed their own dashboards, adapting the framework to reflect their specific circumstances.

At the end of the Commission's term, one of its main recommendations was that more needed to be done at the international level. This message was taken up by the OECD, which took the lead in hosting the follow-on HLEG. But rather than follow through on the full gamut of issues raised in the Commission report, this Group decided to focus on selected issues that had not been dealt with adequately or fully in the initial report.

Thus, this book and its companion volume (*For Good Measure: An Agenda for Moving Beyond GDP*) focus on a selected number of topics, many of which are related to each other: the relevance of the "Beyond GDP" agenda for less developed countries; the distribution of household income, consumption, and wealth; horizontal inequalities among people sharing common characteristics; inequality of opportunity; subjective well-being; economic insecurity; sustainability; and trust. Some of these issues were not discussed in the Commission's earlier report but have since received increasing attention. This is the case, for example, of *vulnerability*, the risk that an economy (or an individual) could fall into a nonsustainable state, and *resilience*, the ability of an economy (or an individual) to recover from an adverse shock. Some issues are old but have become an increasing source of concern: GDP growth cannot continue as it is within our planetary boundaries. Global warming and climate change are real and already upon us, with significant well-being impacts from both weather variability and higher average temperatures, and further effects, such as those associated with sea level rise and changing levels of ocean acidity, not far away. Our indicators must account of these realities.

These subjects were chosen in view both of their importance and of the possibility to develop metrics to measure them. Just listing them conveys their richness and importance for the life of people. The fact that standard metrics have not even attempted to capture changes in these variables helps explain our difficulties in understanding our society and its behavior, and in devising policies that would enhance individual and societal well-being. Several of the topics discussed in this book and the accompanying collection of authored chapters are at the limit of what we can assess with any reasonable degree of confidence. Measurement problems are complex, but that is not an excuse: what we measure is a choice, which reflects implicitly our value system. Not measuring something, even if the measurement is imperfect, has consequences, as we have already noted.

One of the objectives of the report of the Commission on the Measurement of Economic Performance and Social Progress was to highlight the role of metrics in policy, and to instigate a more active dialogue between economic theory, statistical practice, and economic policy, bringing out more clearly the often-implicit assumptions in our statistical practices and their real-world consequences. The same objectives remain central for this book.

Key Changes in the World

The Commission report explained how changes in the economy and society affect both what we want to measure and the adequacy of our metrics. Before the problem of climate change was recognized, there was no reason to measure an economy's carbon emissions. The report also noted that the changing structure of the economy had led to an increasing reliance on imputations—numbers not directly collected by official statisticians but estimated by them in some indirect way.

Since the publication of the Commission report, there have been several changes that heightened the need for (and shaped thinking concerning) a new report. While the Commission was formed before the Great Recession of 2008, this long and deep recession naturally focused attention on the adequacy of our metric system for *assessing the consequences of deep downturns*—in some ways, the original mission of the SNA. It also highlighted the importance of metrics of economic sustainability, indicators showing how an economy might be vulnerable to a major shock.

Higher Economic Insecurity and Lower Trust

The Great Recession had two follow-on effects: a growth of *economic insecurity* and an undermining of *people's trust*, especially in public institutions (which we have already noted). While the Commission had recognized the importance of insecurity and trust, it hadn't done much to propose metrics, or even to explore the conceptual underpinnings of such metrics. It was clear, however, that not taking into account economic insecurity left out one of the main adverse effects of the deep downturn. It was also clear that the weakening of people's trust in public institutions was having social, political, and even economic effects that needed attention, even if no commonly accepted measures of trust had yet been developed.

Rising Inequalities, Global Warming, and Sustainability

Meanwhile, growing concern about *rising inequalities* and *global warming* put an even greater emphasis on *sustainability*, in all of its dimensions. This, in turn, led to the global agreement reached in September 2015 in New York on the Sustainable Development Goals (SDGs), whose overarching objectives are ensuring sustainability and leaving no one behind; and, in December 2015 in Paris, to a common goal of reducing global emissions of greenhouse gases so as to limit the increase in global temperatures to between 1.5 and 2 degrees centigrade.

The SDGs, approved unanimously by the UN General Assembly, were testimony to the power of commonly agreed goals. Fifteen years earlier, the countries of the world had agreed on the Millennium Development Goals (MDGs), a set of goals for reducing extreme poverty by half and raising other aspects of standards of living in developing countries. The attention that the MDGs focused on these commonly agreed goals arguably played a role in the success the international community had in achieving a number of them—though even as they were achieved their limitations were clear: while extreme poverty globally was halved, poverty in Africa remained high. The new SDGs played the role of setting *global norms*, and not just for developing countries but for developed countries as well.

There were intense fights over what to include and not to include in the SDGs. Every NGO wanted the issues for which they were fighting to be included, possibly in the belief that if only more attention were focused on their objectives, more progress would be made. Thus, attempts were made to include some measure of rule of law or even, more narrowly, land titling. The resulting Agenda 2030 was a mix of "ends" and "means to ends," since the ends themselves often proved elusive.

One area in which there was a broad consensus was to set a goal on income inequality.[19] The MDGs had, as we noted, turned the spotlight on extreme poverty, a designation based on the same income threshold across all countries. But, as the SDGs negotiations unfolded, broader concerns came to the fore, not just about those at the very bottom of the income scale. Some worried about the seeming decrease in equality of opportunity, others about the squeezing of the middle class, while still others argued that the large gap between those at the top and everyone else presented a societal problem. These were all different aspects of the distribution of income. Though no single measure of inequality could capture them all, there was a strong case for including *some* measure of income inequality.

As Kanbur, Patel, and Stiglitz emphasize in their chapter in the accompanying volume, the demand for comprehensiveness of the SDGs had an adverse effect: some 17 goals, with 169 targets and 232 indicators, were eventually listed—too many to be meaningfully comprehended or to be a focus of policy. This was not the narrow dashboard that the Commission had recommended. What this implied, the authors suggest, is that countries needed to select which of the goals to focus on, to make them the object of their efforts over the coming years. For most developing countries, that narrow list would almost surely include some measure of employment, of the environment, and of the standard of living of the typical individual—not just GDP. More developed economies are also confronted with the same issue of prioritization. To help them identify where efforts are most needed, and thus establish a limited set of priorities for policy action, the OECD undertook to develop a tool to assess the distance that countries need to travel to achieve each of the SDG targets.[20]

Even when deciding on a broadly defined set of goals, the choice of metrics can make a difference—another of the messages of the Commission. Within any metric are buried assumptions, often quite subtle, about what is important and what is not. We will discuss the measurement of income inequality more extensively below. Here, we simply note that, over time, the shape of the income distribution can change in many complicated ways. Looking at the number of poor people focuses simply on the fraction of the population below a given monetary threshold. The danger of such a measure is that countries can improve it simply by concentrating attention on those just below the poverty line, pushing them across it. In contrast, the poverty gap measures the depth of poverty, i.e., how much income would have to be increased to move everyone out of poverty. Today, however, there is much concern about the squeezed middle class, the reduction of median income, and the fraction of the population that is near the middle of the distribution, say plus or minus 1/2 of median income. To capture these concerns, the share of income that is appropriated by those in the central deciles of the income distribution (or the income ratio between those at the 10th or 1st percentile relative to the 50th, showing the gap between the rich and the rest) seems a more appropriate metric. The SDGs rely on a variety of other indicators, e.g., focusing on the share of income going to the bottom 40%. Others, guided by the observation that the income share received by the middle class was quite similar across a large number of countries, argued in favor of the Palma ratio—i.e., the ratio between the income share of the top 10% of the population and that of the bottom 40%.[21]

While the SDGs are mainly aspirational, they can also be seen as part of an explicit establishment of global norms. All of us want to be part of a "good" society. No one is sure what that means, but when world leaders collectively decide what it means, as they did through the SDGs, it matters—and it provides a point of entry for concerned citizens to press policy-makers to respect their commitments.

In practice, several countries are today organizing their policy agenda around the SDGs,[22] especially the goals that are salient to them, such as those concerning poverty, inequality, and sustainability. Once national goals have been set, countries will want to know how well they are doing, and whether more resources should be devoted to specific areas such as reducing inequality or promoting sustainability. Part of the answer to the question "how are we doing?" is provided by our metrics. That is why the 232 indicators that were agreed upon as part of the SDGs agenda are so important. Of course, as noted above, this does not mean that each country should use a dashboard of 232 indicators, but rather that it should select a limited subset once it has decided on its policy priorities. Ideally, selecting these goals and targets through an open process to assess what society values would deepen a country's democracy and enhance solidarity, trust, and social cohesion.

Changes in Economic Structure

The need for better metrics, particularly on the economic side, is partly related to changes in the structure of our economies. There have been many changes since the SNA was created that affect both its ability to perform its original function—monitoring the state of the market economy—and its usefulness as a measure of economic welfare.

As we observed earlier, the Commission report noted several of these changes. There were, for instance, shifts in many economic activities from the household to the market. As women left the home to work in the labor market, childcare services that previously took place within the home now occurred more frequently within the market. The increase in market activity then exaggerated the growth of production, as it ignored the simultaneous reduction in the production of household services for own use. The benefits of home appliances to welfare may also have been underestimated, because they may have allowed households to enjoy more leisure, whose value is not reflected in GDP. In the United States, the rapid growth of mass incarceration required higher expenditures in prisons that boosted GDP growth but almost surely did not reflect an increase in societal well-being. Similarly, the weakening of the welfare state and the shift in some advanced countries' pension systems from defined benefit systems to defined contribution systems has not only made economies less resilient and more vulnerable to shocks, but has also increased individuals' economic insecurity, as risks are transferred from firms and governments to the people themselves. This has increased the importance of incorporating insecurity into our metrics of well-being, as we have done in this book and, more extensively, in the companion volume.

The Commission report noted two further factors. First, housing has become an increasingly important part of GDP, but the value of housing services is largely based on imputations. It is not just that, with owner-occupied housing, housing services are not a market transaction, but that the SNA imputes what the value of those rents would be if owners had rented their house, based on observation of rents for similar dwellings. As imputations take on a more important role in GDP estimates, the extent to which GDP accurately reflects changes in *market* activity may be reduced.

Second, as goods and services produced by the government are not, for the most part, sold in markets, the value of their output cannot be derived on the basis of market prices but rather on the costs of inputs, which in practice are typically limited to labor. Depending on the methodology used for price and volume measurement, this approach risks underestimating GDP growth when the government becomes more efficient in providing these services. When a labor input measure is used to estimate price and volume changes, efficiency gains will lead to a lower volume of output and value added, and to an underestimation of GDP growth. Although several countries are now using output indicators to measure the volume of government nonmarket production (e.g., for health and education services provided by the government),[23] most still rely on labor inputs when measuring the volume of government production. As the size of the government sector increases, this may result in a downward bias in GDP measures.

Digitalization of the Economy

One change in the structure of our economy, particularly notable in the last decade, which was not discussed in the Commission report, is the emergence of the digital economy. Google, Facebook, and other digital firms seem among the most innovative in the world, and they have garnered for themselves a large share of the increase in global stock market value. Other companies report large efficiency gains permitted by digital technologies and algorithms. The success of these firms has led many to conclude that we are in an "innovative era." Yet aggregate data covering this "innovative era" suggests no reversal in the longer-term slowdown in productivity growth over the last two to three decades in many advanced economies (Figure 1.2). How do we reconcile being in what some call an unprecedented era of innovation with the slow pace of productivity growth? Gordon (2016) suggests that we are not today in a particularly innovative era: the invention of electricity had far more profound effects on our economy and society than the internet did. Indeed, one could argue that much of the profits of these internet giants, stemming in large part from advertising revenues, merely reflects a displacing effect (away from traditional forms of media) that has arguably only a minimal net impact on societal well-being. Others have argued that the pace of technological progress has not slowed down, but that adoption requires changes in organizational structures and business models and that productivity growth naturally lags innovations (Brynjolfsson and McAfee, 2011; Baily, Manyika, and Gupta, 2013).

Some argue that our GDP metrics underestimate the value of the new technologies, because some of their key services are provided for free to users. Google's search engine, for example, has enormous societal value and yet, because access is free, the value of these services does not directly enter GDP (although their advertising revenues do). There are of course good reasons why the value of these services are not directly included in measures of GDP (Ahmad and Schreyer, 2016). As the search is provided for free, its marginal value is zero, and our SNA values goods at their marginal value (the value of the last unit provided), not incorporating "consumer surplus" (the value of all units consumed up to the last). There are other aspects of new technologies that may be of high value, such as the sense of connectedness provided by social media, which are similarly missed by GDP.

On the other hand, critics point out some of the less positive social impacts of digitalization, such as societal polarization and a reduction in people's attention span. Moreover, at the same time that the new technologies provide services of value, there is a reduction in other services of value, such as those that were previously supplied jointly with print media. Consumers have long been accustomed to free newspapers, investigative reporting, and television programs, for example, funded by advertising revenues. That being said, current estimates suggest that the impact of this "exclusion," at least at present, is not significant and cannot explain the slowdown in productivity growth seen during this "innovative era" (Ahmad, Ribarsky, and Reinsdorf, 2017), accounting, at best, for 0.1% per annum of US GDP growth.[24] Where potential mismeasurement related to digitalization may be more important is in the area of prices, particularly in relation to services and new technologies where quality changes rapidly. Even here, however, the impact on real GDP growth and on

Figure 1.2. Productivity Trends

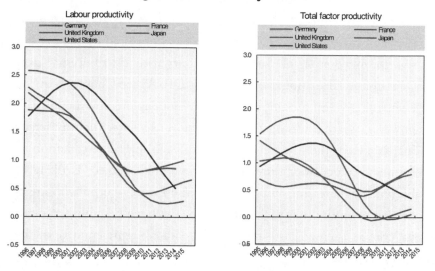

Note: Labor productivity is measured as GDP per hour worked. Trends are estimates using the Hodrick-Prescott filter (OECD, 2018e, *OECD Compendium of Productivity Indicators 2018*, OECD Publishing, Paris, https://doi.org/10.1787/pdtvy-2018-en).
Source: OECD (2018f), *OECD Productivity Statistics (database)*, http://dx.doi.org/10.1787/data-en. StatLink http://dx.doi.org/10.1787/888933842033.

measures of consumer inflation is estimated at most around 0.2 percentage points per annum (Schreyer and Reinsdorf, 2018).

Advances in Data Availability

We have discussed many of the changes in the economy that call for changes in metrics. An important enabler to the development of these new metrics is the availability of new data sets and advances in technology that allow users to rapidly process and analyze large bodies of data and to integrate different data sets. This is a theme that will be repeatedly noted in this book and even more so in the accompanying volume. For instance, indicators of the income of the very rich could be derived from administrative tax returns, and a better picture of the entire income distribution could be achieved by merging numerous administrative data sets (e.g., tax and social security) and survey results. One of the themes explored by the HLEG was the integration of national accounts with distributional data (Distributional National Accounts, or DINA; see Chapter 6 in the companion volume). One of the topics not explored by the HLEG, however, was harnessing the potential of big data, such as scraping data from the internet or exploiting geo-spatial information to form indicators, sometimes in real time. This subject is likely to become of increasing importance in the future—although care is needed to ensure that such data comply with well-established quality criteria, such as ensuring that the data are representative of the entire population.

Policy Implications of "Beyond GDP" Metrics

As we noted earlier, a major impetus for work going "beyond GDP" was to improve policy: what you measure affects what you do. If you don't measure important phenomena, you may not act on them. But distorted metrics can be even worse. When economic metrics don't include the effects of environmental degradation, we have no way of knowing whether a country's welfare is increasing when it expands coal-generated energy, for example. The owners of coal mines might argue that GDP is being sacrificed in the name of the environment if the coal mine is shut down, when in reality, total welfare, correctly measured, would increase when the value of the lost GDP is more than offset by the environmental benefits of cleaner air and the reduced risks of climate change. Similarly, a developing country might allow a foreign company to develop a gold mine within its territory, believing that doing so will increase GDP, while a correct account of the impact of the mine on the well-being of the residents in the country might suggest otherwise. In some (but far from all) countries, better metrics than GDP are produced within the SNA—such as measures of *national* product and *national* income, sometimes *net* of the depreciation of capital goods used in production—that would allow better decisions. But these indicators are not routinely used by those making decisions.

Similarly, some may suggest that privatizing social security will increase GDP as a result of the increased efficiencies and associated savings by households, while a correct accounting of the value of social security could show that the private sector may in fact be *less* efficient than the government in providing these services even when the private sector generates profits, and that privatization may increase individuals' economic insecurity.

One of the key examples we develop later is that, because GDP metrics do not fully capture all of the adverse effects of economic downturns on people's well-being, less may have been done by policy-makers to combat the recession than would have been the case had we had relevant additional or better metrics.

Conclusions

The Commission report, published in English with the title *Mismeasuring Our Lives: Why GDP Doesn't Add Up* (Stiglitz, Sen, and Fitoussi, 2009),[25] not only spurred important work by National Statistical Offices and academics, but also helped to found a global movement, which has taken the form of parliamentary commissions, statistical initiatives involving civil society, and central and local government initiatives to use "Beyond GDP" metrics in their policy determinations. At the international level, one key set of moments of this global movement is represented by the periodic World Fora on "Statistics, Knowledge and Policy" organized by the OECD, bringing together civil society, academics, national statisticians, and government officials to move forward the "Beyond GDP" agenda. There have been conferences in Palermo in 2004, in Istanbul in 2007, in Busan in 2009, in New Delhi in 2012, in Guadalajara in 2015, and in Incheon in 2018, with each meeting gathering more people than the previous one.

A key change that has occurred since the Commission report is the broader acceptance of the need to develop measures of societal welfare, and a stronger appreciation that policies based narrowly on increasing GDP may be misguided.

There were multiple reasons for this increased interest. Environmentalists worried that a focus on GDP resulted in inadequate attention to the environment. And for good reason: current GDP measures pay no attention to resource depletion or environmental degradation. Stiglitz's experience as a member of the US Council of Economic Advisers under President Clinton is telling. Working with the Under-Secretary of Commerce, he pushed to expand the conventional notion about GDP toward a metric of "green GDP" that included resource depletion and environmental degradation. Increased coal production, for example, might add to conventionally measured GDP, but that does not take account of the adverse effects on health from the increased air pollution, or on climate change or on the local environment. Perhaps not surprisingly, the coal lobby struck back, and Congress threatened to cut off financing to the federal agencies undertaking this work if they continued to develop these metrics. These responses made it clear that the coal industry itself believed that what a country measures affects what it does. If a country measures environmental degradation, it is more likely it will do something about it. And that is precisely what the politicians from the coal states did not want to happen.

The same applies in other fields. Those who worried about climate change expressed concerns about the absence of measures on sustainability and resilience—and argued that, without such measures, we would pay insufficient attention to these key attributes of a good economic system.

Those who wanted more active government policies—sometimes involving higher public expenditures—also wanted a change in metrics. As the next chapter will make clear, the costs of recession are not fully captured by GDP. By understating these costs, one is less likely to take strong counter-measures. In the same vein, a focus on government liabilities, without looking at assets, induces excessive conservatism in government borrowing during a recession.

Those who were concerned about social justice, about inequality of outcomes and of opportunity, worried that the focus on GDP had resulted in insufficient attention to "how the pie was sliced." Countries where GDP was increasing but where most people were not doing well were rated as performing as well as those where the benefits of GDP growth were more equally shared. They should not have been.

All these reasons have translated into a large number of measurement initiatives, at both the domestic and international levels. When presenting the Commission report in 2009, President Sarkozy asked INSEE, the French National Statistical Office, to ensure the implementation of the Commission's recommendations at the national level, and the OECD to do the same at the international one, as well as committing his government to bring the Commission's arguments to the attention of the whole international community.[26] The response by the statistical community has gone beyond our expectations, and explains the presence of several official statisticians in the HLEG. These statistical initiatives (which are described in more detail in the Annex) have followed a double track. On the one side, they have aimed at making better use of statistics that already

existed (e.g., on household living standards, inequalities, environmental pressures), bringing them together into dashboards aimed
at providing a comprehensive picture of current well-being and of
its sustainability. On the other side, they have aimed at building the
foundations for new and better statistics on the many aspects of concern to people and communities that are still inadequately covered
by official statistics. Progress in both directions is needed to meet
the Commission's goal to shift the focus of our statistical system
from measuring the volume of economic production to measuring
the conditions of people "here and now" and assuring their sustainability tomorrow.

The response to the Commission report has also gone beyond the
development of new metrics, to explore ways of making systematic
use of these metrics directly in the policy process. As highlighted in
Chapter 4, having a dashboard of well-being indicators is, in some
cases, not enough. What is needed are institutional tools to force
public agencies to act according to the evidence provided by these
indicators, and to overcome the silo thinking whereby each agency
pursues its own narrow goal, without paying attention to how their
actions affect other government departments in their pursuit of their
goals, and with unintended negative effects being recognized only
after the damage has been done. In some countries (e.g., France,
Italy), national parliaments, assigned the task of allocating budgets,
have pushed for better metrics, because they worried that inadequate
metrics would induce wrong budgetary allocations. In others (e.g.,
New Zealand), it was Treasuries that took the lead in developing
broad frameworks—encompassing sustainability, inequalities, and
risks—as tools to help their officials seeking to design policy reforms
or provide advice to other government departments. In other countries yet, policy use of well-being metrics has focused on aligning
priorities and actions across government departments and levels of

administration (Scotland) and on identifying "what works best" in achieving specific goals (the United Kingdom), leveraging the initiatives of various public agencies and actors in the pursuit of higher-level goals.

While all these initiatives, which are described in more detail in Chapter 4, are fairly recent, they share a common ambition: to anchor in policy practice societal concerns that currently don't receive the attention they deserve by policy-makers. The hope is that a discussion of measurement will lead to more democratic engagement around the central questions facing all societies. What do we value? What should we measure? What should we pay more attention to?

2.

The Measurement of Economic Downturns

This chapter summarizes how inadequate metrics (and models) might have affected the assessment of, and response to, the 2008 crisis, and what can be done about it. It argues that GDP may have given an over-optimistic account of how well the economy was doing both prior to the crisis and in the recovery phase, and of the sustainability of growth. The problem was that too many analysts didn't look beyond GDP. If we had had better metrics, including measures that had incorporated more adequately the increases in people's economic insecurity, we might have realized that the consequences of the downturn were deeper than the GDP statistics indicated, and governments may have responded more strongly to mitigate the negative impacts of the crisis. The chapter emphasizes two shortcomings in standard metrics: only looking at government liabilities while ignoring the asset side of the government (and country's) balance sheet, and ignoring measures (broader than the standard unemployment metrics) of the unused resources in the labor market. It stresses the need to complete existing data with measures of economic security and subjective well-being, and to include changes in human and social capital in models.

The statistical data for Israel are supplied by and under the responsibility of the relevant Israeli authorities. The use of such data by the OECD is without prejudice to the status of the Golan Heights, East Jerusalem, and Israeli settlements in the West Bank under the terms of international law.

Introduction

National income accounting began as part of Keynesian economics, as we noted earlier. The hope was that, if we measured GDP better, we might be able to better manage the business cycle and to avoid extended periods of recession. Some also hoped that, drawing from these data, we could build up models to anticipate recessions, and take preemptive action to head them off. So, it is fitting that we begin with an issue within the spirit of these origins. Do our metrics accurately portray the costs or magnitude of downturns, such as the Great Recession? More generally, do they provide the information we need to assess whether the economy is vulnerable to an economic downturn?

This issue is perhaps of particular salience because the Commission report was released only a few months after the default of Lehman Brothers in September 2008, which triggered the financial crisis. The significance of the crisis was present in the mind of the Commission members. They noted that GDP was not a measure of sustainability. In the run-up to the Great Recession, it was evident that US GDP growth had been built on a mountain of private debt, itself partly the consequence of an overvaluation of (real estate) assets, that is a market failure of gigantic proportions. This chapter summarizes how inadequate metrics (and models) might have affected the assessment of, and the response to, the crisis, and what can be done about it.

The Right Choice of Metrics

As seen in Chapter 1, the problems with the information content of standard economic metrics began even before the crisis. Many people thought their economy was in better shape than it actually was. In the United States, where the crisis originated, GDP was growing strongly. Yet, it was clear that much of that GDP growth was produced by a real estate bubble that was leading households and firms to consume and invest more than would have been justified by a more sober assessment of market conditions; and that some of the US government's strong fiscal position was a result of tax revenues garnered as a result of that real estate bubble.[1]

Though GDP may have given an over-optimistic account of how well the economy was doing, and whether growth was sustainable, the real problem was that too many analysts didn't look *beyond* GDP.[2] A dashboard of indicators such as the one suggested by the Commission, including measures providing accurate information on financial fragility, would certainly have helped. But, more fundamentally, analysts and decision makers should have abandoned the ideological blinders that stood in the way of getting a good understanding of how the economic system works.

When there are symptoms that the economy might be in a real estate bubble, say, when the ratio of median housing prices to median income is abnormally high,[3] then one might want to look more closely at a set of indicators of the financial health of the economy and of its banking system. Real estate bubbles are associated with rapid increases in bank lending. A simple analysis of the fraction of households who might face difficulties in refinancing their mortgage, or who might not have incentives to repay their loans in the event of a significant fall in house prices, would have shown the economy's financial fragility.[4]

This illustrates that care must be exercised in the choice of the relevant indicators. Some analysts looked at average house prices compared to the average level of household indebtedness: if all households were the same, the crisis would not have occurred, for even a large fall in prices would not have put the mortgages at risk. But there was (and normally is) a large dispersion in the distribution of (net) home equity among owners, and when there are many homes with little equity it doesn't take much for many homes to become "under water"—that is, with a value of the mortgage exceeding the market value of the house, thereby exposing households to the risk of default. And if banks are excessively highly leveraged, it may not take many mortgages to default to result in banks being undercapitalized. Most of the data needed to make these assessments—which would have indicated that the US economy was indeed in a precarious position—were available before the crisis, even if in some cases they were not as timely as it would have been needed; but there was no "crisis dashboard" to which policy-makers or ordinary citizens could turn. In its absence, most market operators (and experts) were happy to believe all was well, and that market prices could not significantly depart from "fundamentals."[5]

Standard economic theory contributed to the failure to assess the risks confronting the economy in important ways. Macro-economics models focused on "representative agents" ignore the distribution of assets and liabilities among them—essentially assuming that distribution does not matter. This theory implied that all one needed was data for the average. Also, while the standard models did not have a rich theory of the financial sector, to the extent that finance was incorporated, it was with a "representative bank." Such an approach, of course, ignored the risks posed by financial inter-linkages among banks, and the possible consequences of a bankruptcy cascade, where the failure of one financial institution (like Lehman Brothers) would lead to further failures. Of course, economic theorists had warned precisely of this kind of risk well before the crisis (Allen and Gale, 2000; Stiglitz and Greenwald, 2003).

Here, however, we wish to focus on what happened *after* the crisis, i.e., in assessing the magnitude of the effects of the economic downturn. The thrust of our argument is that, if we had had better metrics, including measures that had incorporated more adequately the increases in people's economic insecurity, we might have realized that the depth of the downturn was deeper than the GDP statistics indicated; and if that had been the case, perhaps governments would have responded more strongly to mitigate the negative impacts of the crisis.

Recent research has also shown how our econometric models underestimate the decrease of GDP during recessions[6] and the strength of future growth prospects (Stiglitz, 2014, 2016a, and 2016b). Often (depending on the model used) this is because we systematically underestimate the decrease in wealth (or capital) due to the destruction of, or lower investment in, economic, human, and social capital—both that resulting directly from the downturn,[7] and that arising indirectly from inappropriate policy responses. These types of capital deliver both market and nonmarket benefits: they are important for sustaining people's well-being in general, but also as drivers of future GDP growth.

Missing Wealth

That something had happened to total wealth as a result of the Great Recession became evident in the years following the onset of the downturn. Figure 2.1 shows the level of GDP per capita from 1991 to 2019 for the United States and euro area, respectively, based on a simple extrapolation of pre-crisis performance for the period after 2009. The continuous line shows the actual levels of real GDP per capita (with OECD forecasts for the years 2018–19) while the dotted line fits a (linear) curve based on historical data (1991–2006); "diamonds" show the annual percentage difference between actual and projected GDP per capita in each year, while "squares" refer to cumulative differences since 2009.

While different extrapolation models may give different measures, the obvious point here is that there is an enormous gap between where the economy is and where it, presumably, might have been based on previous trends.[8] The gap is larger for the euro area than for the US but is significant in both cases. How can we account for this gap?

The factors at work are many. In both the United States and the euro area there was a decline in labor input, especially in the years immediately following the crisis. Investment, as measured in the national accounts, also declined, leading to less capital accumulation and lower physical capital per worker. In crisis-afflicted countries, cutbacks in public investment were particularly significant, with potential adverse effects on countries' future economic prospects. Similarly, there were often drastic cutbacks in private investments, both because of the pessimism about future prospects and uncertainties and because the economic downturn adversely affected firms' cash flow, and weaknesses in the financial system reduced the supply of loans, both of which diminish investment among cash-constrained firms. In the aftermath of the crisis, forecasted GDP growth in crisis-affected countries was typically overestimated by international organizations and private companies, typically by a large margin, one of the reasons being that the decrease in investment was underestimated. Again, those responsible for policies in the aftermath of the crisis do not seem to have taken fully into account the knock-on effect of these policies on private investment and future economic prospects.[9]

But one simply cannot account for the difference between observed GDP and the GDP that could be "predicted" based on past historical performance on the basis of changes in labor inputs and physical (economic) capital. There is also some "missing capital," i.e., changes in human and social capital that we normally do not take account of in macro-economic models, and that are key drivers not just of people's well-being but of long-term GDP growth as well. And indeed, there may have been decreases in both types of capital, and of a significant amount.

Figure 2.1. Actual and Projected GDP per Capita, the United States and the Euro Area

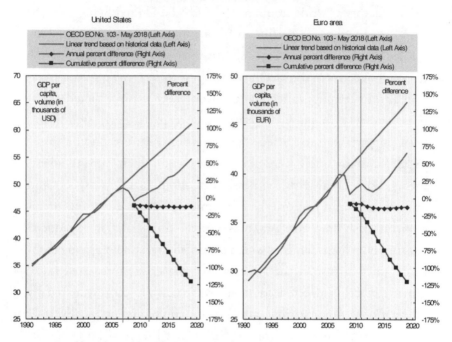

Note: Trend based on 1991–2006 data. Data for the euro area are limited to OECD member countries excluding Lithuania. Data on GDP per capita (volumes) in 2018 and 2019 are based on OECD projections.
Source: OECD (2018a), *OECD Economic Outlook*, Volume 2018, Issue 1, OECD Publishing, Paris, https://doi.org/10.1787/eco_outlook-v2018-1-en. StatLink http://dx.doi.org/10.1787/888933842052.

Human Capital and Knowledge

The easiest change to see—and to understand as something that we typically fail to take account of—is the change in human capital.[10] While statistics on human capital typically focus on formal *education*, learning on the job is just as (or perhaps) more important. This includes in-work training provided by firms to workers, but also the accretion of skills that occurs simply from having a job. When there are high levels of unemployment, especially youth unemployment, large numbers of people are simply not learning: there cannot be as much learning-on-the-job when large fractions of the population do not have jobs. Indeed, even those with high levels of skills will find that those skills decline when they remain unemployed for long periods. Models that estimate the amount of learning that occurs from having a job and from being on the job longer would enable us to get an estimate of the loss of this human capital. We can get some inkling of the magnitude of these losses by looking at what happens to those (typically young people who completed their education) who enter the labor force in a recession. The lower wages and higher unemployment experienced by new graduates who enter the labor markets during recessions lead to "scars" that permanently affect their careers. They are likely to have significantly lower lifetime incomes compared with cohorts who entered the labor market during phases of expansion (Garrouste and Godard, 2016; Kahn, 2010; Oreopoulos, von Wachter, and Heisz, 2012).[11]

In crisis-affected countries, formal schooling was affected too, but in less visible ways. While the share of public expenditure in GDP increased marginally (on average and in most OECD countries) from 2008 to 2014, it declined (by 0.2 point or more) in countries most affected by the crisis such as Italy and Spain (Figure 2.2, top panel). Of course, when considered in absolute terms, the decrease in public education expenditure was larger, as GDP was falling or increasing by less than before the crisis. The effect of the crisis on private expenditures on education is more ambiguous: cash-constrained households cut back spending on education, but many young people stayed in school for longer, as fewer jobs were available—i.e., the opportunity cost of education is lower. In Italy and Spain, the reduction in public spending in education simply shifted the costs to households, whose private spending increased.

Overall, the recession may have led to a regression in the state of *knowledge*, including institutional knowledge held within organizations/firms, and studies have shown that such knowledge accounts for a large part of multi-factor productivity growth (OECD, 2013a). The bankruptcies that abound in an economic downturn lead to a destruction of this institutional knowledge. Even when knowledge is not destroyed, the pace of creation of new knowledge is reduced, as both public and private investments in knowledge are reduced. Because the effects of cutbacks in such investments will only be felt years later, it is often far easier to make cutbacks in these expenditures than, say, on the wage bill. This shows the importance of developing better metrics of human capital that encompass all forms of knowledge, and to take this into account in conventional "growth accounting" models.[12] This issue is discussed in more detail in the chapter by De Smedt, Giovannini, and Radermacher in the companion volume.

Another important aspect of human capital is *health*. Whether or not the economic crisis and the macro-economic policies implemented in its aftermath had an effect in worsening the health conditions of the population in the affected countries is an issue debated by researchers, including HLEG members. On the one hand, a plausible case can be made that individuals who lose their jobs may suffer adverse mental health effects, partly because of the emotional effects of unemployment, including stress. Long periods of unemployment can also have particularly large adverse effects on people's health, and give rise to a vicious cycle, with poor health leading to poor job prospects and low incomes, reinforcing weak health. Similarly, cutbacks in health services in some European countries resulting from austerity policies (most notably in Greece) may have long-run effects on the health of the population (Kentikelenis et al., 2014). There is also some evidence that these health consequences directly affect economic performance years after the crisis (IMF, 2013). The US low labor force participation rate is in part explained by the poor health status of a large fraction of those not in the labor force, with nearly half of them being on prescription pain medication (CEA, 2016; Krueger, 2017).

On the other hand, other empirical studies have failed to detect a significant effect of the recession on health conditions. Most OECD countries experienced higher spending (as a share of GDP) in both public and private health-care spending (Figure 2.2, bottom panel).[13] In the United States, the decrease in life expectancy among middle-aged whites, which mainly affected low-educated people due to what Case and Deaton (2015) refer to as "deaths of despair," started well before the crisis, and does not appear to have intensified since then. And while most OECD countries experienced a decline in life expectancy in 2015, it represented a unique occurrence—the decline

Figure 2.2. Public and Private Expenditures in Education and Health-Care as a Percent of GDP

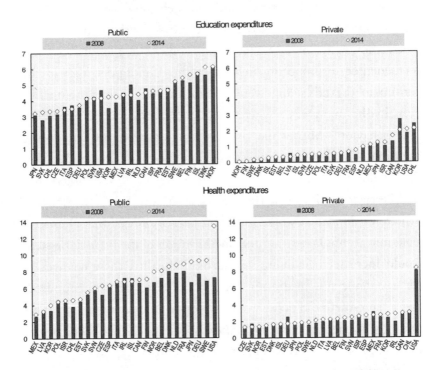

Note: Data on health spending for the United States refer to 2013 instead of 2014.
Sources: OECD (2017c), OECD Education Statistics (database), https://doi.org/10.1787/1c1c86c4-en and OECD (2017d), OECD Health Statistics (database), https://doi.org/10.1787/828a6dbd-en. StatLink http://dx.doi.org/10.1787/888933842071.

reversed in 2016—and was concentrated among the elderly (who had already exited the labor market), mainly reflecting an unusually strong wave of influenza epidemics (EuroMOMO, 2018). More data and research are needed to monitor these changes in health conditions and associated inequalities, as well as to identify their drivers.

Social Capital

One category of "missing" capital that has received insufficient attention is social capital, in particular trust in institutions. A deep downturn is, in itself, evidence that our economic system is not managed well. In any society, management of the economic system is entrusted to a political and professional elite. But in a downturn the members of that elite tend to keep their jobs, while other individuals don't. This was particularly the case in the United States, where those with management responsibilities in the financial sector benefited disproportionately from the economic system in the run-up to the crisis, but were not in any way held accountable, even in the many cases where they engaged in socially reprehensible behavior.[14] Meanwhile, ordinary citizens were not only losing their jobs, but also their homes and more. To many, it appeared that the economic system was "rigged" to benefit a few. Workers and middle-class families saw themselves as hardworking, yet reaping little reward for their work. They had been promised that globalization, new technologies, and the liberalization of the financial system would increase their living standards. In reality, these changes in the economic system did not lead to the faster growth promised, and what growth did occur went disproportionately to the top. This not only implied growing inequality, but it was also followed by the most serious crisis in three-quarters of a century.

Even the recovery may have given rise to a decrease in trust, with politicians declaring the end to a recession even as most continued to suffer its consequences. In short, there were multiple reasons for the loss of trust in the economy and in institutions. Later in this book, we will describe more fully the relationship between trust and economic performance. Here, we simply note that this loss of trust can be thought of as an erosion of social capital, another part of the explanation of the "missing" capital. Having an accounting system that could reliably trace changes in economic, human, and social capital would provide the basis for a better understanding of the costs of economic downturns—which in turn could induce governments to take more resolute actions in responding during a recession.

Economic Security and Subjective Well-Being

The "missing capitals" that we discussed above can be understood as drivers of both people's well-being *and* GDP growth. Beyond these effects, however, there are several other ways in which our system of economic indicators does not adequately reflect the true consequences (i.e., the costs) of recessions.

For instance, we observed earlier that an important aspect of individual well-being is economic security. Individuals spend large amounts of money to buy insurance against many of the risks they face. Markets, however, fail to provide insurance against some of the most important risks, like the loss of a job. In response, governments have provided a variety of forms of social insurance, most notably unemployment insurance, which is based on the idea of pooling risks among different groups of workers. In a number of European countries, as well as in the United States, unemployment benefits were increased in the earlier years of the crisis to cushion the negative-income impact of the increase in unemployment. But in most countries, unemployment insurance covers only a fraction of those who don't have jobs, and does not cover those entering the

labor force, who may have spent large amounts of money and invested considerable time in the hope that education would enable them
to get a suitable job.[15] And very few countries provide insurance
for underemployment, as in the case of self-employed people who
see their incomes contract as their salaries get reduced. In addition,
because of the lack of adequate insurance, some people may also lose
their homes when their earnings fall. Few countries have designed
mortgages that enable individuals to postpone repayments in periods when they have lost their jobs.

The longer a recession lasts, the greater the cost for people's economic security. Better measures of economic insecurity would have
shown the large losses caused to individuals by the crisis in this
respect.

More broadly, individuals' sense of well-being fell sharply in the
countries most affected by the recession,[16] and especially so for those
who lost their jobs or for young people who didn't get one. People
who become unemployed report lower life-evaluations, even after
controlling for their lower income. These adverse effects persist
over time. The unemployed also report higher prevalence of various
negative experiences (sadness, stress, and pain) and lower levels of
positive ones (joy, contentment, optimism). These subjective experiences suggest that the costs of unemployment exceed the income-
loss suffered by those who lose their jobs, reflecting the existence of
nonpecuniary effects associated with unemployment, and the fears
and anxieties generated by unemployment in the rest of society.

Research has provided what might seem obvious explanations for
these patterns. Individuals look to work as an important part of their
identity and sense of worth. Someone who cannot support their
family loses face with themselves, their family, and those they asso-
ciate with. Being connected to others is also important for people's
sense of well-being, and the workplace is one of the main sources of

connectedness in our society. Individuals who lose their jobs thus feel more isolated, and more unhappy (De Neve, 2018). Measures of subjective well-being, the importance of which were emphasized in the Commission report, would have indicated this.

Economies Never Fully Recover from a Deep Downturn

In short, had policy-makers relied on a dashboard of indicators, which reflected more broadly what was going on in the economy and society, they would have realized the severity of the economic downturn for well-being. The decline in the "true wealth" of the country should have been of particular concern in those countries most afflicted by the crisis such as Greece, Spain, Ireland, Italy, and Portugal, as it undermined their economic potential in the future.

Economies that experience deep downturns may *never* fully recover. Figure 1.1 and Figure 1.2 illustrate what is at stake. Even when GDP growth returns, it is never sufficiently strong to close the gap between where the economy was and where it would have been. And even if growth returns to its pre-recession rates (without closing the original GDP gap in levels), the present discounted value of the loss is enormous.[17]

Beyond the effects of the crisis on the *level* of GDP, there is a debate on whether the long-term effects of a deep recession also extend to its future *growth rate*. Recent research has suggested that, while economies never recover to the pre-crisis level of GDP, the long-term growth rate is unaffected.[18] This is what we should expect from standard growth theories, where the pace of technological change is exogenous to the system (i.e., "manna from heaven"). But, as we argued above, deep downturns affect human capital and impair a country's capacities to invest in research, which may affect growth for an extended period of time. Note that Figure 2.1 shows that rates of GDP growth post-recession in both the United States and the euro area are lower than prior to it. While the growth slowdown started before the crisis,[19] the crisis may well have intensified it. The real estate bubble burst two years before the crisis, and its full impact took time to be felt. Moreover, distortions associated with the crisis, with excessive resources going into real estate, would themselves undermine a country's long-run growth potential. More fundamentally, whether the economy might *eventually* recover its growth rate may not be as important as the question of how long it takes. The longer it takes, the greater the cumulative value (discounted) of the loss. Interventions that more quickly restore the economy to full employment may, accordingly, reduce the cumulative loss by a substantial amount.

The Misuse of Existing Metrics: A Misplaced Focus on Government Liabilities

The other side of the coin when discussing the implications of our measurement system is the cost of *responding* to the crisis. An inappropriate use of statistics may have led many countries to overestimate this cost. A standard tool for managing the business cycle over the past three-quarters of a century has been an increase in government spending, which, in a deep economic downturn with high levels of unemployment, can generate an increase in GDP that is a multiple of the original spending (Blanchard and Leigh, 2013). This is especially the case when such policy is put in place through concerted action of different governments.[20] But in economic downturns, tax revenues are down and, especially in countries with more developed social safety nets, public expenditures are already high, so that fiscal deficits increase. Government spending, unaccompanied by increases in taxes, naturally leads to further increases in the public deficit. Some governments, focusing narrowly on this increase in public deficit and debt, argued against responding to the downturn with more government spending. Indeed, in Europe, a strict interpretation of the Stability and Growth Pact would require that euro-area governments keep their deficits below 3% of GDP even during a recession—although de facto many euro area countries exceeded the 3% limit as a consequence of the crisis, and a number of them have public debt levels above the 60% target.[21] Whatever their merits in providing the basis of sustained long-term growth and mitigating cross-border financial and economic problems within the euro zone, it is clear that the deficit and debt limits hamper the functioning of automatic stabilizers (the tendency for public deficit to increase when growth falters), just as the very moment when those stabilizers are most needed. In practice, the enforcement of the constraints has converted government fiscal policy from being counter-cyclical to being pro-cyclical, exacerbating economic downturns, an effect that was most evident in crisis-affected countries.

This focus on government liabilities is, we would argue, another example of a misuse of data. What matters for the country as a whole going forward is the nation's balance sheet, along with balance sheets of all institutional sectors, i.e., households, private companies, the government, and the rest of the world. The balance sheet looks at *both* assets and liabilities. If the increased government expenditure takes the form of higher investments—whether in people, technology, or infrastructure—its balance sheet should not deteriorate, as assets and liabilities increase by the same amount. It is simply a mistake to look only at the liability side of a balance sheet. No analyst would do that in looking at the economic prospects of a firm. Neither should we when we are looking at government.

There is, however, a major difference between the balance sheet of the government and that of a firm (or household). The firm doesn't capture the multiplier effects of its increased spending on its own revenues, while the government does. If a firm borrows money to buy an asset, its balance sheet improves if and only if the return on the asset exceeds the cost of capital. (Of course, households typically face a higher cost of capital than the government, putting the threshold rate of return still higher.) But this does not apply to the government's account, which will also benefit from the higher tax revenues generated by the fiscal expansion. Especially in a deep downturn (when multipliers are large and interest rates are low), the government's balance sheet position might improve even when the return on investment is below the interest rate on government debt.[22]

It might be argued that the picture is less bright when the government cannot appropriate the returns of its investment. But even in this case, the balance sheet for the country as a whole should be improved by this investment. Broadly speaking, whether it pays for a country to borrow from abroad depends on how it invests the funds. If it borrows abroad for current consumption, then the country balance sheet worsens, and the prospects of future generations deteriorate, absent any macro-economic effects. Conversely, if it borrows to finance high-return investments, the country's balance sheet improves. For example, the criticism of the higher amounts that the United States as a whole borrowed abroad every year—as reflected in the current accounts deficit being above 5% of GDP in the years before the crisis—was that, at the margin, much of the spending was for consumption and for low-yield investments, such as building shoddy homes in the middle of the Nevada desert. When that happens, the country's balance sheet deteriorates.[23]

There is another reason for taking a comprehensive view of the balance sheet position of all sectors of the economy, beyond the government. This is because large deficits and debts for the country as a whole may reflect household and firm deficits and debt, even when the government's fiscal position is seemingly sound. In a crisis, these private debts often morph quickly into public debts. This is especially the case with bank liabilities. We saw this happening in the case of Ireland, where bank debts guaranteed by the government quickly changed the government's fiscal position from a debt-to-GDP ratio of less than 30% in 2007 to one that was over 130% in 2012.[24] In most cases, this shift in liabilities from the private to the public sector is a result of domestic political pressures, as when the politically powerful financial sector puts pressure on the government to bail out banks, arguing that otherwise the whole country would suffer. Though there is now a consensus that such arguments are specious—the government should not bail out shareholders, bondholders, or bankers, but only (where necessary) assume liabilities to protect depositors—and some governments like that of the United States have enacted legislation to thwart such bail-outs in the future, the reality is that, especially when there are banks "too big to fail" (or too interconnected), there will be bailouts.

Accordingly, in assessing the government's financial position, one should look beyond the government's balance sheet, and make some assessment of the risk that private liabilities will become public liabilities in the future. This is precisely why the G20 Data Gaps Initiative includes a recommendation to record transactions that take place between the different economic sectors (households, private companies, government, and the rest of the world) to detect when financial weakness in one sector can spill over to another.

Constructing Capital Accounts

Today, few governments construct these general government and national balance sheets. Information on financial assets held by governments (such as cash balances, equity holdings, and the value of government participation in state enterprises) and by other sectors of the economy is typically available, but this doesn't apply to non-financial (i.e., real) assets, such as infrastructure networks, schools, and health care centers.

There are also issues on the liabilities side. Beyond the government liabilities that are recorded on the government balance sheet, off-balance liabilities may stem from contractual obligations of the government (e.g., commitments to pay pensions to its former employees or to jointly invest with private partners), contingent liabilities associated with guarantees provided to financial institutions, and implicit liabilities which, while not having a contractual form, represent a "promise" to citizens (and other institutions) to provide benefits in the future.

Still other issues arise relating to the distinction between general government and other public-sector entities (such as central banks and state enterprises). These are important because of the close interactions between these entities and the government, especially in the case of vehicles created to deal with troubled financial institutions (Barnes and Smyth, 2013). This is a form of the "debt transfers" from the private to the public sector discussed above.

The implementation of some of the recommendations of the G20 Data Gaps Initiative would give a better picture of what is happening to a country's overall wealth and the government's financial position. It does not, however, go far enough, because not all forms of capital are currently considered. More comprehensive balance sheets can be constructed on the basis of currently available data, though in doing so judgments would have to be made. One such judgment is where to draw the "asset boundary." Today, structures (bridges, buildings, etc.), equipment (machines), research and development spending, and land and subsoil assets are all within the asset boundary of national balance sheets (although rarely fully measured). Other assets could be brought into those boundaries, for instance, human capital—the result of expenditures on education and training—or functioning ecosystems that may have been helped by expenditure on the environment.[25] Most health expenditures, especially on children, should also be included as investments.

National accounts experts have been discussing these issues for many years, and the reason for their omission is, in most cases, not one of principle but of pragmatism: new assets are only included when robust and comparable measures can be developed and data are available.[26] There are likely to be disagreements about how best to treat each category of government expenditure, and about how rapidly the investment made may depreciate in the future.

These problems must and can be overcome, with data generated to support the creation of more comprehensive national and sectoral balance sheets. As a principle, items considered as investments should be treated more favorably than those that are not, especially in an economic downturn when funds are short.

Responses to Government Deficits and Debts

The previous paragraphs explained why conventionally measured deficits and debts provide only a partial view of the government's true net worth and of its changes. A repeated message of this book is that what you measure affects what you do. When public assets are not fully measured, while its financial liabilities are, there is undue focus on the liability side of the government's balance sheet. The same applies because of incomplete capital accounts and national balance sheets. This has contributed to policy stances, such as that of the euro area Stability and Growth Pact, limiting government deficits to 3% and debts to 60% (numbers that are the result of a political process rather than a calculation based on economic theory or strong empirical evidence). Government deficits increased in the Great Recession as a consequence of automatic stabilizers (the natural tendency for government expenditure to rise, and for taxes to fall, when the economy weakens) and of the expansionary policies adopted by some countries in the period up to 2010. But these policies were then reversed due to concerns about higher public debt. With the onset of the euro crisis, some countries lost access to funds, and were forced to adopt extreme policies of austerity—cutbacks in government expenditure—which exacerbated the economic downturn and the hardship associated with it. Even in countries like the United States, which had easy access to funds, expansionary policies were severely constricted; at least part of the reason was an excessive focus on the wrong metric.

Thus, while austerity was not an inevitable consequence of the reliance on a misguided set of statistics, the latter contributed to the hardship imposed by the crisis and to its long-run consequences.

Unemployment: A Partial View of Available Labor Resources

Most of the discussion in this book is on the measurement of people's welfare, and of the limits of GDP when used as a proxy of it. But other statistics, some of which need to be part of the dashboard of indicators by which to judge how well the economy is doing, need to be looked at with equal caution. Consider one of the primary indicators of an economic downturn, the level of unemployment.

Unemployment is typically measured by surveys, asking individuals whether they were not at work in the reference week of the survey, actively seeking employment, and available to start work if a job was found. If they meet all these conditions, they are counted as unemployed. But, especially as the economy goes into a deep downturn, this approach may give an overly rosy view of the depth of the recession.

When individuals have been looking for a job for months and don't find one, they often give up looking. They become "discouraged workers." They are not unemployed according to the criteria listed above, but surely they are not employed either. Also, many are forced to take a part-time job when they would prefer to work full time. Broader measures of unemployment, which include discouraged workers and those involuntarily working part time, show a far higher level of unused labor resources (Figure 2.3). There are other adjustments that could be made to give a better picture of the true status of the labor market. Some individuals who can't get jobs claim disability benefits, since these are usually higher than unemployment benefits.[27] These people may well be suffering from a disability, but when a decent job is available they manage to overcome their disability and work. Many individuals who would like a job decide to get further education (as noted above) and halt their job search. While this may increase human capital, the measured unemployment rate would in any case underestimate the weakness in the labor market by excluding these people.

Figure 2.3. Unemployment and Labor Underutilization

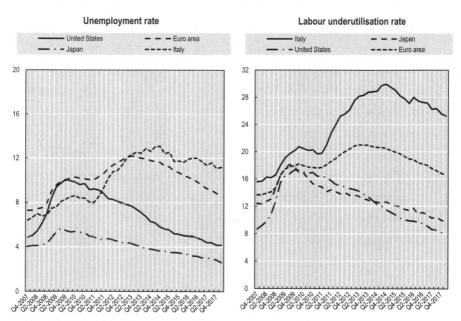

Note: The labor underutilization rate includes in the numerator the unemployed; persons not in the labor force who did not look for work during the past four weeks but who wish and are available to work; full-time workers working less than usual during the survey reference week for economic reasons; and part-time workers who could not find full-time work, expressed as a ratio of the labor force.

Source: OECD (2018d), *OECD Labour Force Statistics 2017*, OECD Publishing, Paris, https://doi.org/10.1787/oecd_lfs-2017-en. StatLink http://dx.doi.org/10.1787/888933842090.

Part-time work presents still another measurement problem. According to international standards, a person is classified as employed even if working only one hour a week. But many workers in a recession work fewer hours than they wish. In many respects, then, a better measure of the state of the labor market may be the total number of hours worked.[28]

Deep economic downturns can have, as we have noted, particularly severe effects on particular groups. In many OECD countries, the unemployment rate of youth increased by roughly twice the rise for the population as a whole (Figure 2.4). Disadvantaged groups were particularly adversely affected: in the United States, the unemployment rate of African Americans increased by roughly twice that of the country as a whole, and that of young African Americans increased by four times. Indeed, the only time when the unemployment rate of African Americans came down to what might be viewed as an acceptable level was in the late 1990s and then in 2007, when it fell to around 8%. High unemployment rates among these groups is particularly of concern, because it increases societal divides, an issue that we discuss below.

While progress has been made by the statistical community in improving the measurement of labor market slack (see Annex), these measures still fail to capture the attention of politicians and the media to the same extent that the standard unemployment rate does. One consequence is that we may have an overly optimistic picture of the state of the labor market than what is warranted by reality.

Conclusions

History matters. In 2008, at the onset of the global financial crisis, the hope was that, once banks had restored their balance sheets, the economy would return to normal. GDP growth would then resume from where it was and the economy would make up for what was

Figure 2.4. Unemployment Rates by Age

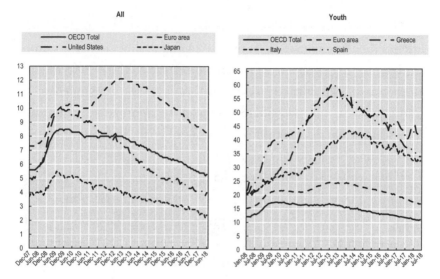

Source: OECD (2018d), *OECD Labour Force Statistics 2017*, OECD Publishing, Paris, https://doi.org/10.1787/oecd_lfs-2017-en. StatLink http://dx.doi.org/10.1787/888933842109.

lost in the intervening years. This has not happened. Even in the United States, where the unemployment rate has come down markedly, the level of GDP is far below what it would have been in the absence of the crisis: there is no sign of making up for lost time.

The destruction of "hidden wealth" described in this chapter was one of the legacies of the 2008–09 recession. This destruction will have long-lasting effects, and explains part of the gap between where the economy is today and where it would have been in the absence of the crisis. The "hidden wealth" that determines the future levels and change of productivity can be estimated, and its components better understood, with the objective of identifying policies that might mitigate its fall. For instance, the destruction of future productivity might be reduced through sharing the limited amount of work that is available during a crisis, as Germany did. But even comprehensive measures of human, social, and physical capital may not fully capture the effects of a deep downturn on society, i.e., its effect on how people think, feel, and act.

The experience of the Great Depression and the Great Recession exemplifies the importance of having a good dashboard of indicators with which to evaluate what is going on in the country, to formulate appropriate economic responses, and to assess the consequences of those policies. The dashboard that may be appropriate in normal times may have to be modified in times of crisis, to monitor closely and respond to fast-changing circumstances.

The human costs of the crisis have been large, and some of them are missed by conventional statistics. In most countries, while GDP growth is now back or close to pre-crisis levels, the economy will never return to where it would have been without the crisis. In many advanced countries, the recession had the effect of depressing productivity growth and capital accumulation relative to what it would otherwise have been. Even without taking into account the full cost of human suffering, the long-run costs of the recession to people's well-being have been enormous.

There is a chance that a more adequate set of indicators, reflecting the true depth of the downturn and its long-term economic implications, would have allowed governments to respond more forcefully, with special attention to those parts of the population that were feeling the full brunt of the recession. And it may well be the case that reliance on the wrong indicators, with governments announcing a recovery when large fractions of the population were not experiencing any improvement in their well-being, contributed, at least partly, to the distrust in public institutions and the rise in discontent and anti-globalization sentiments that we are witnessing today throughout the world.

3.

The Need to Follow Up on the Stiglitz-Sen-Fitoussi Commission

This chapter looks at work carried out since the 2009 Stiglitz-Sen-Fitoussi Commission on going "beyond GDP." It argues that the 169 targets agreed on by the international community on the Sustainable Development Goals are too many, and that countries have to select a set that corresponds to their priorities. It shows that growing inequality in income and wealth are global concerns and that, even in developed countries, data are often inadequate. It warns against over-reliance on broad averages, since these fail to reflect important inequalities across given groups ("horizontal inequalities") and say nothing about how resources are shared and managed within households. The chapter argues that what matters are not just inequalities in outcomes but inequalities in people's opportunity to achieve those outcomes, and that measuring this is possible. Other areas where more work is needed include subjective well-being and economic insecurity, which interact with social capital and trust, as well as sustainability across its social, economic, and environmental dimensions.

The statistical data for Israel are supplied by and under the responsibility of the relevant Israeli authorities. The use of such data by the OECD is without prejudice to the status of the Golan Heights, East Jerusalem, and Israeli settlements in the West Bank under the terms of international law.

Introduction

While much has been happening since the Stiglitz-Sen-Fitoussi Commission's report in 2009 in terms of high-level national initiatives, statistical production, and research, it was also clear that greater focus and more work were needed in a number of areas. Five years on, the decision was therefore taken to create a follow-up High-Level Expert Group (HLEG) hosted by the OECD to take stock of progress, to provide direction and maintain momentum, and to identify new areas requiring more work. The HLEG decided to focus on nine broad areas: the Sustainable Development Goals (SDGs), including global and developing country perspectives; income and wealth inequalities; horizontal inequalities, i.e., inequalities among groups of people sharing the same characteristics; the integration of information on economic inequalities in macro-economic statistics; inequalities of opportunities; subjective well-being; economic insecurity; sustainability and resilience; and trust. While authored chapters on each of these topics are included in the companion volume, we provide below our own perspective on these issues.

Sustainable Development Goals: How to Measure Progress in Poorer Countries

In Chapter 1, we noted that one of the major changes since the report of the Commission in 2009 was the agreement by the international community on a set of SDGs, a global norm–setting process applying to developed as well as developing countries. These goals, endorsed by the UN General Assembly in 2015, expanded the range of goals well beyond the Millennium Development Goals that had been formulated in 2000 as aspirations by the development community to be achieved by 2015 (Table 3.1). The SDGs entail ensuring shared economic and social progress as well as environmental, social, and economic sustainability.

Table 3.1. From the MDGs to the SDGs

Millennium Development Goals (MDGs)	Sustainable Development Goals (SDGs)
1. Eradicate extreme poverty and hunger. 2. Achieve universal primary education. 3. Promote gender equality and empower. 4. Reduce child mortality. 5. Improve maternal health. 6. Combat HIV/AIDS, malaria, and other diseases. 7. Ensure environmental sustainability. 8. Develop a global partnership for development.	1. No poverty. 2. No hunger. 3. Good health and well-being. 4. Quality education. 5. Gender equality. 6. Clean water and sanitation. 7. Affordable and clean energy. 8. Decent work and economic growth. 9. Industry innovation and infrastructure. 10. Reduced inequalities. 11. Sustainable cities and communities. 12. Responsible consumption and production. 13. Climate action. 14. Life below water. 15. Life on land. 16. Peace, justice, and strong institutions. 17. Partnership.

The goals were increased from 8 to 17, with 169 associated targets. The goals focused the attention of both policy-makers and citizens on issues deemed important by the international community. As the former UN Secretary Ban Ki-moon said: "They [the MDGs] generated new and innovative partnerships, galvanized public opinion and showed the immense value of setting ambitious goals. It was hoped that the SDGs would perform a similar role" (United Nations, 2015).

The proliferation of goals reflected the inevitable tension between, on the one hand, the pull to broaden and expand indicators for assessing and monitoring economic and social progress, and, on the other, the imperative to keep a relatively small number of indicators at the "top level of the dashboard," in order to facilitate national discourse and policy-making. Of course, the more information is detailed and the greater data are disaggregated, the more complete the picture one has of what is going on. But limited human attention requires that indicators be streamlined, and this is especially so if the statistics are to influence the public debate. The Commission "squared the circle" by arguing for a dashboard of indicators. However, the 169 SDG policy targets, and 232 indicators for "global monitoring" agreed by the international community, are clearly too many.

Focus is especially important for developing countries, where resources—including the human resources necessary to design and implement the policies required to achieve the goals and to develop the large number of indicators to monitor progress—are limited.

Given that different countries face different circumstances, it is natural that they will and should focus on different objectives. Differences are likely to be especially significant between developed and developing countries. For example, while most of the former have managed to achieve relatively high rates of formal employment and low levels of extreme poverty, lack of productive employment and poverty are still of central concern to most developing countries. But there is a cost to having different goals pursued by different countries—it undermines intercountry comparability. Countries themselves need to be mindful of the benefits of comparability: to know how well one is doing, one wants to know how well other similarly situated countries are performing. Still, it is likely that many similarly situated countries will choose similar goals.

Metrics

Even when the set of goals is settled on, the choice of metrics can make a difference—another of the messages of the Commission—and the metrics that developing countries might want to focus on may well differ from those of the more developed ones.

In the case of SDG 1 ("End poverty"), for example, the indicator agreed by the UN Statistical Commission for Target 1.1 ("By 2030, eradicate extreme poverty for all people everywhere") is the number of people living below the $1.9 per person per day global poverty line.[1]

Most developed countries are likely to have met this target already: poverty generally means something markedly different in the developed world.[2]

Or consider SDG 10 ("Reduce inequality"). The indicator chosen for Target 10.1 ("By 2030, progressively achieve and sustain income growth of the bottom 40% of the population at a rate higher than the national average") is the growth rate of household expenditure or income per capita among the bottom 40% of the population. Jose Gabriel Palma of Cambridge University has argued that a more sensitive measure of income inequality, especially for emerging economies and developing countries, is the ratio of the income share of the top 10% of population divided by the share of the poorest 40% (Palma, 2016). He argues that the income share of the middle class seems relatively similar across at least middle-income and developing countries, so that this ratio really identifies the differences across countries. Doyle and Stiglitz (2014) argue, therefore, that the Palma ratio might be the preferred measure of income inequality for the SDGs.

Measures, of course, embrace values and concerns. Target 10.1, advocated by the World Bank, is a more inclusive measure than extreme poverty, but is still in keeping with the Bank's traditional focus on the lower part of the distribution.

Global Policy Issues

One important issue raised by Kanbur, Patel, and Stiglitz in their chapter of the companion volume relates to metrics for matters of global concern. Most importantly, we need to know what is happening regarding climate change (which requires measuring the *global* carbon emissions from the economic activities of a country, i.e., both those relating to the production within its borders and those associated with a country's imports to satisfy its domestic demand). There is also a great deal of interest in knowing what is happening to *global* income inequality (the inequality that we would observe if we ranked all people in the world by their income, as if they were living in the same country), especially in assessing the offsetting effects of higher within-countries inequalities and lower income disparities across countries (Deaton, 2013; Milanovic, 2016). There is value in having National Statistical Offices collect data on a sufficiently comparable basis so that we can make reasonable estimates of what is happening in both regards.

Inequalities in Income and Wealth

At the time of the Stiglitz, Sen, and Fitoussi (2009) report, we were intensely aware that one of the reasons that GDP was not a good measure of economic and social performance was that it took no account of distribution: a society in which most people were doing poorly, but a few were doing very well, was not, in a fundamental sense, a well-performing economy, even if GDP was increasing, possibly even rapidly. Indeed, that was the case for the United States and in most other advanced countries. Using GDP as a metric, the US economy seemed to be doing reasonably well. But looking at measures that took into account distribution provided a markedly different picture. The United States, as some commentators put it, was a great country in which to be born, if you knew you were going to be in the top 1%, or even better, in the top 0.1%; being born in the bottom 90% was a markedly different story.

In the years since the Stiglitz, Sen, and Fitoussi report, the attention paid to income inequality has increased significantly, partly thanks to the availability of new data showing the long-term nature of this rise and the increasing share taken by the 1% (Piketty, 2014); and partly driven by the sheer size of the increase in income inequality that has taken place since the late 1970s. Comparative data analyses have also shown cross-country differences in the size of this increase in inequality, which suggests that country-specific factors, and in particular policies and institutions, matter considerably.

Income inequality, its causes, consequences, and what should be done about it have thus become a focus of policy discussions around the world. This is a new and important development, which also reflects the contributions of several of the members of the HLEG (Fitoussi and Rosanvallon, 1996; Fitoussi and Stiglitz, 2013; López-Calva and Lustig, 2010; Bourguignon, 2012b; Stiglitz, 2012a; Piketty, 2014; Deaton, 2013; Atkinson, 2015) and international organizations (OECD, 2008, 2015; IMF, 2017; Ostry, Berg, and Tsangarides, 2014). Research has highlighted a number of drivers of income inequality and of its increases over time, which include both changes in the structure of the economy (globalization, skill-biased technological change, the more important role of the service sector, especially the financial sector, and the higher market power of firms in many sectors) and weaker bargaining power of workers, itself a function of some of the other changes noted. Changes in policy affect the distribution of both market and disposable income. These include changes in the rules governing labor markets, corporate governance, and globalization and anti-trust; changes in policies affecting the inter-generational transfer of advantage and disadvantage, such as inheritance taxes and public education; and policies affecting redistribution through taxes and transfers (Stiglitz, 2015; Inchauste and Lustig, 2017). In all cases, however, policies to reduce inequalities will require gathering better data, and incorporating more systematically into policy deliberations an analysis of the effects of alternative policies on the distribution of income and wealth.

The Stiglitz, Sen, and Fitoussi report emphasized not only the importance of inequalities in income and wealth, but also of every other aspect of well-being: health, education, political voice, insecurity, access to justice, opportunity. Many of these inequality indicators are correlated, with the same households or individuals experiencing disadvantage in many of these dimensions. The report argued that one should focus on the household (or even better, the individual) as the unit of analysis, looking at all the dimensions that affect well-being at the same time. Dashboards need to take into account what is happening, say, to average health outcomes, but also who is in good or bad health. The Case-Deaton study (2015) referred to earlier highlights this issue: even if longevity is increasing and mortality decreasing on average, just the opposite is happening among American whites who have only a high school education, and this is the same group that has seen their incomes plummet. (The same issues arise in making cross-country comparisons.)

Growing Inequality in Most Advanced Countries

For more than 30 years, while the income gap between major emerging markets (e.g., China, India, and Brazil) and advanced countries was narrowing, the gap within most, but not all, advanced countries was rising. According to OECD data, 18 out of 23 OECD countries experienced a significant increase in income inequality between the mid-1980s and around 2013 (OECD, 2015a, p. 24). In some cases, the increase in inequalities in market income was offset by government tax and transfer programs. In others, most notably the United States, it was not, resulting in figures that could only be called alarming. By 2017, the median family income adjusted for inflation was barely above the level it was a quarter-century earlier, real wages were barely above the level attained 60 years earlier, and the real median income of a full-time male worker was lower than 41 years previously.

While the United States was the most extreme case, others were not far behind. OECD studies showed that there were large increases in income inequalities even in countries like Sweden that had earlier established a reputation for egalitarianism, though even with their large increases in inequality, their income inequality was far lower than for others. The rise of income inequality was also important in most emerging countries.

A Global Perspective

Branko Milanovic combined what was happening within and between countries into a global picture (Milanovic, 2016). A single diagram, reprinted below (Figure 3.1), summarizes much of the story. Two groups have been doing very well, the global top (point D in diagram), i.e., the 1%, and the emerging middle-class in China and India, around the 50th percentile (point C). These two groups have been the main beneficiaries of globalization. There are two groups, conversely, who did not do well: those at the bottom, e.g., people in conflict-affected areas or subsistence farmers in developing countries (point A), hurt in part by European and American agricultural subsidies; and the working/middle classes in Europe and America (point B), especially those with limited education.

Figure 3.1. Cumulative Gains in Real Income Growth Around the World, 1988–2008

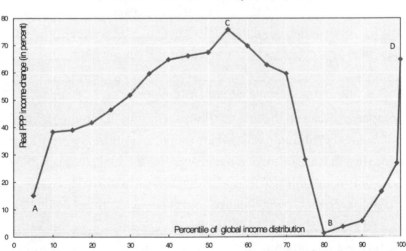

Source: Milanovic, B. (2016), *Global Inequality: A New Approach for the Age of Globalization*, Harvard University Press, Cambridge, MA. StatLink http://dx.doi.org/10.1787 /888933842128.

Using the standard metric for measuring inequality, the Gini coefficient (see the discussion below), we see that the effect of reduced cross-country inequality and increased within-country inequality largely offset each other.[3] But summarizing Figure 3.1 into a single number such as the Gini coefficient misses much of the story—the discontent among the middle class in the advanced countries and among those at the bottom of the income pyramid, and the outsized gains of the very wealthy.

Milanovic's data may be affected by a range of assumptions and measurement problems (Kharas and Seidel, 2018),[4] and do not give a full picture of the extent of variability in levels and changes in income inequality across countries. Income inequality (by most measures) is not only higher in the United States than in other advanced countries, it has also increased the most. In several OECD countries, the increase in inequality was concentrated in the early 1990s, while in Germany the increase started in the early 2000s and in France in the late 2000s (Bourguignon, 2012b). Some countries in Latin America even saw income inequality reduced, albeit from a high level. In some countries like China, a massive reduction in poverty has been achieved alongside higher income inequality—with the rich experiencing greater income gains than the poor.

Some Broad Data Issues

Comparative data on income distribution for OECD countries[5] exist today, but they did not exist when the long-term "wave" of higher inequality started (in the United Kingdom, the United States, New Zealand) in the mid-1970s and early 1980s. Had these data been available back then, policy-makers and concerned citizens could have noticed the trend and might have taken action to counter it. While the increase in economic inequality was noted earlier in individual countries, this was often dismissed as reflecting country specifics. In reality, the common pattern to higher economic inequalities became more evident and common across countries, partly the consequence of the same set of policies that had been introduced in the United Kingdom and the United States in the late 1970s and early 1980s being adopted elsewhere. Income inequality became an area of concern long after the damage was done.[6]

Data on economic inequalities are today often weaker in those countries where they are most needed, for instance in those emerging and developing countries that are experiencing strong economic growth *unequally shared*, without the cushion provided by adequate social protection programs. As documented by Nora Lustig in the companion volume, while various data on economic inequalities for these countries exist, they are often based on estimates made up by researchers. Even when good, quality official micro data exist (e.g., China), access to them is often out of reach for both researchers and international organizations. Also, most data on economic inequality in developing and emerging countries are based on surveys of consumption expenditures rather than income. When countries grow rapidly and household savings increase (for those households that benefit from growth), the increase in consumption inequalities will be less than the increase in income inequalities. Similarly, as these countries undergo a process of urbanization and demographic transition, growth of household income and consumption *per capita* may exceed growth of household income and consumption *per consumption unit*, due to lower household size. On both accounts, policymakers in these countries may be underestimating the increase in economic inequalities because of inadequate data.

Even in rich countries, out-of-date measures of income inequalities are a problem, with such data typically lagging *by years* the most recent data on GDP. Data on income inequality have little traction in policy discussions simply because, by the time the data become available, they represent "water under the bridge," and often reflect policy decisions taken by previous administrations.

Limits to the metrics used in national official statistics on economic inequality can bias policy discussions, as some examples illustrate. While, for purposes of measuring inequality, the broader metric of income inequality is that of *adjusted* disposable income (which includes the individual services provided for free, or at subsidized prices, by governments to households), most of the available measures of income inequality are typically based on cash income. While there are methodological challenges in measuring in-kind services, their exclusion from the income metric often allows policymakers to get away with the "fiction" that tax cuts improve people's economic well-being even when they are offset by cuts in valued public services. Similarly, some developing countries have devoted significant expenditures to help the poor through better education and health care programs. These programs improve the well-being of poor children, but do not show up as an increase of the cash income of beneficiaries.[7] Over time, they should lead to higher incomes, moving people out of poverty, but these income effects take time to show up.[8]

Statistics on the distribution of household economic resources remain limited in other respects.[9] First, traditional surveys on the distribution of household income have come under increasing scrutiny because of their failure to capture development at the top end of the distribution. Other sources (mainly tax records) have been increasingly used, in particular following the work by Atkinson and Piketty (2007) and their co-authors. Use of administrative data sets has prompted questions about the role of each source, their strengths and limitations, and possible ways to integrate them. Tax records typically don't have adequate representation of those at the bottom end of the distribution, while there is some presumption that the incomes of those at the top are understated—in some cases as a result of employing legal loopholes, in other cases as a result of more questionable practices bordering on tax evasion. In some countries, the rich shelter much of their income through corporations, and so income that rightly should be attributed to them is not. In most countries, capital gains are reported in tax declarations (if reported at all) only when an asset is sold.[10] Indeed, when capital gains are given tax preferences (as is often the case), rich individuals have found easy ways of converting what otherwise would be a dividend into a capital gain. At the other end of the distribution, even surveys, which do a better job than administrative data in picking up incomes at the very bottom, are inadequate (Atkinson, 2016). Surveys miss the homeless, people in institutions and jails, or those with no permanent address.[11]

Second, there are typically large differences in levels, and sometimes changes, in income inequalities, on one side, and inequalities in consumption expenditures and wealth, on the other. Administrative data can provide good income measures, subject to the limitations discussed above, but we have to rely on surveys when it comes to measuring consumption expenditures. Measuring consumption, rather than income, has both advantages and drawbacks. On the one hand, individuals may be better able to report what they consumed (through diaries) than the income they have received: for example, "net income" for a small shopkeeper who does not keep books is an abstract concept, and reported numbers may be inaccurate. On the other hand, individual-level data on consumption have their own limits: they are burdensome to report for survey participants, implying that results may miss the very poor; they may omit expenditures on durable goods or, when they include them (often in a separate module), record them as consumption expenditure flows that should, in theory, be distributed over several years.[12] These data are also affected by their own measurement errors, due to factors such as the length of the recall period, the number of consumption items listed in the diary, and whether participants record their consumption themselves or are interviewed.[13] Especially troublesome is the fact that we may have data only for income inequality in some countries and only for consumption inequality in others, making cross-country comparisons difficult.

Third, the treatment of government-provided goods and services is especially problematic, as these items may represent a large fraction of the "effective consumption" of low-income individuals. Ignoring such goods and services may give a misleading view of levels and changes in both economic inequality and average living standards. The problem (to which the 2009 Commission report called attention) is that because these are not market transactions, it is hard to value them, and in some cases, hard even to identify who are the recipients. Medical services are especially difficult to value for noninsured people; but even for those covered by health insurance, valuing the transactions at market prices is unsatisfactory, since market prices are generally distorted. In many countries, such as the United States, the cost of providing health care services has risen much faster than the cost of living in general. The result is that, even when nominal health spending is increasing faster than the CPI (consumer price index, which is the overall measure of cost of living), real health services may be actually falling if one used a health-care specific price index. This is important: Burkhauser, Larrimore, and Simon (2012) noted, using income metrics in nominal terms, that inequality in living standards in the United States was increasing by less than claimed, once one takes into account the large increase in (nominal) health care expenditures. However, accounting for the higher increase in health care prices would lead to the opposite conclusion.

Fourth, we still lack adequate data on the distribution of household wealth. This lack is especially troublesome at a time when many rich countries have been reducing taxes on wealth holdings, capital income, capital gains, and inheritances (OECD, 2018b). The regressive implications of these policies are not given adequate weight in policy discussions, partly because adequate data on wealth distribution are not available.[14] In addition to the problems described earlier on the measurement of income, there are two more critical limitations in the case of household wealth data. First, in some countries, significant amounts of the wealth are held abroad, including in tax heavens. While Zucman (2015) has shown the large magnitude of this hidden wealth, incorporating it into countries' wealth distribution data is a huge challenge. Second, in some countries wealthy people may hold significant fractions of their wealth in trusts and foundations, the beneficial ownership of which is often not transparent. Since the fraction of the wealth so held can vary markedly across countries, this makes it difficult to make cross-country comparisons of wealth inequality. Similarly, the fraction of wealth so held can vary markedly over time, especially with changes in regulations and tax laws.[15]

Last, micro-statistics on household income, consumption, and wealth (even when they exist) are only rarely collected in a joint way, with information of each component available for each household.[16] A stronger correlation between different types of economic resources would imply higher economic inequality even when the (marginal) distribution of each type is unchanged. As noted earlier, the natural unit of analysis is the household, or the individual, and those at the bottom typically suffer deprivations in all dimensions. Evidence on the joint distribution of income, consumption, and wealth for the United States suggests that their correlation has increased over time, meaning that "true" economic inequality has increased faster than when looking at each type of economic resource separately (Fisher et al., 2016). For most other countries, we simply don't know the magnitude with which figures were underestimated. Recent OECD work on the joint distribution of income and wealth shows for instance that more than 40% of people in OECD countries lack the liquid financial assets that would prevent them from falling into poverty if they had to forgo three months of income, indicating widespread vulnerability to unforeseen economic shocks (Balestra and Tonkin, 2018).

Technical Issues

Beyond these issues, a host of important technical issues have to be addressed when comparing economic inequality both across countries and over time. There are, for instance, many issues affecting the comparability of data, which in turn affect the ability to make cross-country comparisons. There are also differences in the nature of data sets between advanced and developing countries, and in the extent to which the data provided by respondents correspond to appropriate definitions of income or consumption. For advanced economies, economic inequality is typically measured based on *equivalized* income (where adjustments are made for family size and sometimes for the age of each household member), while for other countries consumption or income *per capita* is more commonly used. Large differences across countries and over time in household size raise questions about cross-country comparisons of income inequality. In some developing countries, the very notion of the household (people sharing the same roof and meals) may be difficult to define and measure.

While in principle the income variable that should be the focus of attention when analyzing inequalities is *disposable income* (what individuals can spend, after paying their direct taxes and receiving any current transfers), the precise income concept used by respondents in most Latin American countries (where surveys have traditionally measured income rather than consumption) is often not clear. Likewise, while international standards in this field (UNECE, 2011) argue that both income and consumption should include goods produced within the household for their own use (services produced within the household, such as child care, are excluded due to the difficulties in measuring them) as well as imputed rents of owner-occupied housing (the rent that individuals would have had to pay if they were renting their house), in practice this is not in general the case, even among industrialized countries.[17]

Similarly, the impacts of consumption taxes and subsidies on household economic resources are typically neglected. As shown in the chapter by Nora Lustig in the accompanying volume, while it is generally acknowledged that household consumption possibilities are reduced/increased by consumption taxes/production subsidies passed on to the prices that households pay for the goods and services they purchase, taking this impact into account has not been part of the conventions typically used for analyzing disparities in households' economic well-being and for analyzing the redistributive impacts of government taxes and spending.[18] Fiscal incidence studies that take these taxes into consideration highlight significant distributive effects (Lustig, 2018).

Secondary databases differ too on whether adjustments (and which ones) are made to the underlying micro data in order to correct for underreporting, to eliminate outliers, or to address missing responses on specific items. This situation results in inconsistencies between data sets, meaning that different data sets may produce different estimates about the level of inequality even when the underlying data source is the same. In some cases, these problems may be so large that ascertaining whether there has been convergence in levels of inequality among countries may simply depend on which secondary data set is used.

Describing Income Inequality: The Choice of Indicator

Presenting (and summarizing) data on inequalities in income also gives rise to a number of problems. The usual summary statistic is the Gini coefficient, an index which varies between zero (in the case of perfect equality, i.e., everyone has the same income) and 1 (in the case of perfect inequality, i.e., all the income accrues to a single person). This index is computed based on a Lorenz curve (Figure 3.2) that plots cumulative shares of the population against the cumulative shares of the income received (e.g., people in the bottom 10% of the population may receive 5% of total income, people in the bottom 20% may receive 12% of total income, etc.). The Gini coefficient is twice the area between the Lorenz curve and the diagonal, and corresponds to the average income difference between all pairs of individuals in the sample.

However, only when the curve for one year is below that for another year at all points in the distribution can it be said that a higher

Figure 3.2. The Lorenz Curve for Income

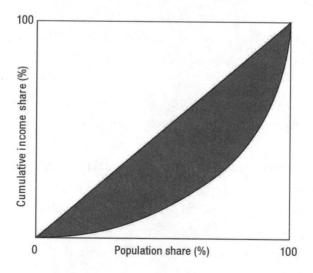

Gini coefficient indicates an unambiguous increase in inequality— that is, all inequality-averse societies would prefer one curve to the other. Whenever these curves "cross" each other, the assessment of changes in income inequality depends on the "weight" attributed to different portions of the curve. For instance, some societies might be more concerned with the hollowing out of the middle class, others with the 1% seizing such a large fraction of the nation's economic pie, and still others with the depth of poverty. Even when these curves do not cross, for policy purposes it is important to know what is happening to each part of the income distribution—to those at the bottom (living in poverty), to those in the middle (the middle class), and to those at the higher end (the top 1%). Inequality measures capturing developments at different points of the distribution should be routinely reported alongside measures summarizing the overall distribution.

Sir Tony Atkinson introduced in 1970 a welfare-based measure that assessed, given society's concern about inequality, the loss in societal well-being that is due to income inequality (Atkinson, 1970). This measure asks how much income people would be willing to give up if it could eliminate all inequality. With reasonable assumptions on the degree of "inequality aversion," the welfare-loss turned out to be quite large (up to a third or more of their average income). But even this measure may underestimate the "price of inequality," for it focuses on eliminating *all* inequality. The relevant question, in most cases, is how much a country would be willing to pay to get rid of *some* inequality, i.e., as elsewhere in economics one wants a *marginal measure*. Stiglitz (2009) developed one such measure, showing that it typically is much larger than the Atkinson measure; but unlike the Atkinson measure, applications have been fewer to date.

Using Inequality Metrics in Policy Design

In many areas of regulation—e.g., those concerning the environment and safety—it is common to require a cost-benefit analysis, to force policy-makers to assess both the benefits of the regulations and their costs. Likewise, it should be routine to require for any major policy an assessment of its distributional consequences, as the IMF has now started doing.[19] It is conceivable that, if such procedures had been routine, there might not have been the large cuts in capital gains taxes in the United States under President Clinton, which contributed so greatly to the growth in inequality; and if there had been a cut, it might well have been designed differently.[20] It is also possible that such assessments would have led to some second thoughts about the austerity policies imposed on some European countries following the financial crisis. Similarly, it would be advisable to assess the distributional impacts of changes in labor market regulations. For example, changing a labor market regulation without providing adequate social protection and active labor markets programs might generate adverse impacts on inequality out of balance with any positive efficiency gains.

Macro- and Micro-Level Statistics on Household Economic Resources

The System of National Accounts originated out of the need to have the information necessary to manage the economy following the Great Depression, and was based on Keynes's notion that governments could use monetary and fiscal policy to manage the economy. Both the impact of income distribution on macro-economics and the impact of macro-economic policies on distribution were often not well recognized, and even less frequently taken into account in policy discussions, especially over the past four decades.[21]

This has changed today. A range of studies since the crisis (mainly undertaken by researchers at the IMF and OECD), based on cross-country data sets combining data on GDP growth and income inequality, have suggested that higher income inequalities may have reduced GDP growth (Ostry, Berg, and Tsangarides, 2014; Cingano, 2014). This negative interpretation has some plausibility in the aftermath of the 2008 crisis, when lack of demand was a key constraint on growth, owing to different propensities to spend by people at different levels of the distribution.[22] But there are obviously huge data problems for any research that combines micro and macro data that are measured on the basis of different concepts and that exhibit large differences in how the data change over the same period. The difficulties are even larger when it comes to assessing the direction of causality between the two and the role of other factors in explaining their association.

At the same time, the unorthodox monetary policies (quantitative easing) used by central banks to support the economy in the aftermath of the crisis had large (adverse) distributional impacts. Retired individuals who held safe short- and medium-term bonds saw their incomes hurt because of low interest rates, while wealthy individuals who owned a disproportionately large share of equities saw the value of their stocks soar as a result of markets' positive response to quantitative easing. This distributive effect, largely offsetting or more than offsetting the distributive benefits from higher employment, which had been one of the objectives of these monetary policies, may have contributed to limit the effectiveness of these policies in sustaining growth and contributed to a sense of unfairness in the design of public policy, fueling people's mistrust in government.

It is thus clear that macro-economic and distributional data need to be integrated. Macro- and micro-statistics on household economic well-being have historically developed on parallel tracks, sometimes leading to very different conclusions on how household living standards had, on average, changed over time. Macro- and micro-consistency is obviously important, and the disparity in numbers should call attention to the deficiencies in each source. Scholars have been aware of the large discrepancies for some time (Altimir, 1987; Deaton, 2005; Anand, Segal, and Stiglitz, 2010) and have suggested ideas to explain the reasons behind them. However, coordinated action at the international level to put macro- and micro-data on household economic resources on a consistent framework started only in 2011, when the OECD and statistical office of the European Union (Eurostat) carried out a feasibility study on compiling distributional measures of household income, consumption, and saving within the framework of national accounts on the basis of micro data. By working to obtain consistency, we may get a far more accurate picture of what is going on. Research reported by Alvaredo et al. in the accompanying volume highlights the progress that has been achieved in harmonizing the two sets of data, through harmonized definitions and methods, and in using national accounts, surveys, and tax data together with other data sources such as rankings provided by "rich lists" compiled by the press.

While most analyses of the rise in income inequalities are based on summary inequality measures, which are based on surveys, assessment of the *pace of income growth* for people at different points in the distribution has to contend with the large (and growing) differences in measured income growth that are reported in micro and macro sources. All attempts to bring together information on both sources have to confront a range of controversial methodological issues (described by Alvaredo et al.) and to make choices that are open to disagreements. That said, when these choices and assumptions are made, these estimates highlight some of the markedly different patterns across the world. For instance, the estimates reported by Alvaredo et al., which combine data from tax, survey, and macrodata sources, show that between 1978 and 2015 national income per adult increased by over 800% in China, by around 60% in the United States, and by around 40% in France. In China, the average income of the bottom 50% also grew strongly, by around 400%, but less than the average, hence inequality increased. In contrast, the bottom 50% of the population in the United States experienced a small income drop (–1%). In France, the income of adults in the bottom half of the distribution increased at the same pace as the average, and income inequality was broadly stable—with only small increases in the second half of the 2000s.

The integration of macro and micro statistics on household income, in ways that are consistent with macro-economic totals for GDP and its components, is necessary to reach firmer conclusions about the relationships between macro-economic activity, policy, and distribution. An understanding of these relationships is important not just because macro-economic policy may have unintended distributional consequences, but also because economic inequalities matter for the transmission of monetary and fiscal policies, and for assessing risks of default linked to changes in asset prices. Macroeconomists simply cannot ignore issues of distribution in the way they did in the past.

Horizontal Inequalities

Vertical inequalities such as those discussed above describe the extent of differences between, say, the rich and the poor. Horizontal inequalities describe differences among roughly similarly situated individuals or groups, e.g., between men and women, across races or ethnic lines, or within the family. Horizontal inequalities are often associated with discrimination, which has well-discussed moral, social, political, and economic consequences. Horizontal inequalities among different groups can lead to political instability when the groups on the losing side manage to build coalitions according to their shared identities (Doyle and Stiglitz, 2014). It is possible, even likely, that had more attention been paid to horizontal inequalities, conflicts based on ethnic or religious groups might have been avoided or at least lessened. At the same time, data showing the magnitude of horizontal inequalities can confirm existing beliefs about discrimination, thereby heightening tensions.

Some types of horizontal inequalities are more difficult to capture than others. Traditional settlement countries have long-established methods of data collection that look at race and ethnicity, while in many European countries (those scarred by the experience of genocide and discrimination during World War II, or those that only recently experienced large-scale immigration) such types of data collection are either explicitly forbidden or still underdeveloped. A case can be made that, by not collecting these data, these countries are blinding themselves to the most severe forms of discrimination.

Some of the criteria for comparing horizontal inequalities across countries also lack well-established statistical conventions and definitions. An example is provided by disability status where, despite decade-long discussions, no generally accepted definition applied across official surveys exists yet. In other cases, no statistical criteria exist simply because these types of horizontal inequalities (for example, those linked to sexual orientation) have only recently entered public discussions: it is important that such definitions are agreed and implemented in the context of population censuses.

Other types of horizontal inequalities are better understood but raise specific issues in terms of measurement. In particular, focusing on household economic resources doesn't tell us how economic resources are distributed *within* the family or household, and whether there are systematic gender biases. We know that there are inequalities in the distribution of resources within families, especially in poor societies where girls are less likely to receive education, or even food or health care, than their male siblings. In more developed countries, we also know that the identity of the family member who receives the welfare payments affects how these benefits are shared within that family (Woolley, 2004; Browning, Chiappori, and Weiss, 2014).

Deere, Kanbur, and Stewart, in Chapter 4 of the accompanying volume, argue that inequality is underestimated when intra-household inequality is not taken into account (see also Deaton, 1997). However, as we have noted, gathering the requisite data to assess intra-household distribution is not straightforward. Indirect indicators such as marital regimes, or information on the weight or stunting of different household members, may provide information on within-household inequalities in some contexts. In most circumstances, however, measuring intra-household inequalities will require distinguishing between those income streams that are paid to each household member (e.g., earnings) and those that accrue jointly to all (e.g., returns on family assets), who in the family makes the most important financial decisions, or the part of individual income that is not shared with other members. Collecting information on both individual and household economic resources in the context of the same survey would help to develop better (if still imperfect) measures of gender inequalities, and help to target a range of policies (e.g., whether welfare payments are paid to the male or female partner in a couple) to reduce them.

Inequality of Opportunity

Inequalities in the distribution of household economic resources and other individual characteristics are not the only type of inequalities that matter to people and communities. In fact, many observers claim that what matters are not inequalities of *outcomes* but inequalities of *opportunity*. In a fair society, everyone should have equal chances to achieve good outcomes regardless of the circumstances of his or her birth. Prominent politicians have claimed, for instance, that while the United States has more inequality of incomes than other countries, it has more equality of opportunity. This is an empirical claim, one that needs to be supported. To ascertain the answer to that question, one needs a conceptual framework—how should equality of opportunity be defined—as well as metrics and data with which to make the assessment.

Inequality of opportunity may be defined as the differences in the set of options available to individuals and/or families in different circumstances. Thus, an important strand in the economics literature attempts to distinguish between an individual's circumstances and their efforts. Equality of opportunity, in this approach, means that individuals exerting the same levels of effort should have the same outcomes (or the same probability distribution of outcomes) regardless of their circumstances.[23] In particular, it would mean that individuals born into poor families who exert a given level of effort would have as great a chance in succeeding in life as those born to a rich parent exerting the same level of effort.

Unfortunately, as shown by Bourguignon in Chapter 5 of the accompanying volume, we typically do not observe effort. What this means in practice is that differences in outcomes that are not explained by observable circumstances are attributed to effort. If these circumstances explain only a small fraction of outcomes, there is a presumption that there is a high level of equality of opportunity.

In fact, if differences in circumstances significantly shift the probability distribution of outcomes for a given level of effort, then it is not possible to disentangle what is due to one and what is due to the other. Moreover, our ability and willingness to exert effort may itself be affected by the circumstances of birth. So the conceptual distinction between circumstances and efforts is, at best, blurred.

Why Do We Care?

People care about equality of opportunity because it is unfair, because it is inefficient, or because of both. Most people feel that children are not responsible for the circumstances of their birth, and many would find it deeply unfair if a child's life chances were found to be determined by those circumstances. Inequality of opportunity is economically inefficient because it generates disincentives, undermines morale, and is associated with a misallocation of resources. Individuals who perceive that outcomes are largely predetermined by the circumstances of their birth have little incentive to exert effort. A perception that the economic system is rigged, that those born at the top will be the winners, will also lower morale. (This is sometimes referred to as the fairness-efficiency wage effect.) If part of the inequality of opportunity is associated with a lack of access to education or other resources, then it implies that those at the bottom of the scale will underinvest in it. All of these factors imply that inequality of opportunities leads to a less efficient and a more unequal society.

Indeed, inequalities of opportunity will lead to the perpetuation of inequalities of outcomes. Most of the inequalities in income and wealth of the present generation (which are an essential determinant of the set of opportunities of their children) transfer themselves to the next generation. In turn, inequalities of the latter generation become inequality of opportunities of the following generation. Thus greater inequalities in one generation are translated to the next. The process is cumulative. In the words of Alan B. Krueger: "The rise in inequality in the United States over the last three decades has reached the point that inequality in incomes is causing an unhealthy division in opportunities, and is a threat to economic growth. Restoring a greater degree of fairness to the US job market would be good for businesses, good for the economy, and good for the country."[24]

Corak (2013) documented the systematic relationship between inequalities of opportunity and inequalities of outcomes.[25] He showed that societies with greater inequality of outcomes systematically had lower levels of economic mobility. This is reflected, for instance, in data suggesting that the children of rich Americans who do poorly in school wind up having higher incomes than children of poor Americans who do well in school (Bartik and Hershbein, 2018). It is not effort (or even intelligence) that determines outcomes so much as the circumstances of birth.[26]

One of the important implications of this analysis is that, while conceptually clear, the practical demarcation between equalities of opportunity and equality of outcomes is fuzzy. Fortunately, as the discussion below highlights, statistics already available provide some guidance on policies that could increase equality of opportunity.

Metrics

While the Commission in 2009 emphasized the difficulties in measuring inequalities of income and wealth, those presented by inequality of opportunity are far greater. A standard, roughshod approach is simply to measure the correlation between the earnings of a child and that of his or her parents (typically the father) at the same age (Corak, 2013). Equality of opportunity is then measured by the size of the correlation between the two. When on average there is no correlation, earnings mobility across generations is high, and it is said that there is a high level of equality of opportunity. Knowing at least one key circumstance—the parents' earnings—provides in this case no information about the child's prospects. In reality, in many other countries (OECD, 2018c), the correlation is high.

But this approach does not give us the kind of information that we would need to identify the source of the failure in equality of opportunity. A society could be marked by poverty traps, even if on average there is a reasonable level of mobility. An often-used approach looks at the mobility matrix, which describes, say, the probability for someone whose parents are in the middle-income deciles of moving up or down to the top or bottom quintile. Such a mobility matrix can show the presence of a poverty trap, where someone in a low-income decile has a small probability of significant upward mobility, even if someone in a middle decile has more mobility.

With sufficient data, one can refine the correlation analysis described above, asking what the correlation is between the parents' income (and education) and that of the child with parents in the bottom, middle, or top of the income distribution.

One of the key problems with implementing these ideas is the absence of data, and this is an especially important limitation if one wants to ascertain long-run trends. Ideally, we would like to know the relationship between the lifetime income of somebody today and that of his or her parents, and that between the parents and the grandparents, requiring data on income stretching back decades in time.[27] With less data, one can ascertain the income of an individual who is, say, 40 years old and then compare it with that of his or her parents when they were 40. But if the profile of earnings is changing over time, and in ways that differ at different income levels, correlations between children' outcomes and parental characteristics will become less informative.

Of course, intergenerational advantages and disadvantages may be transmitted not just by income, but by a broader set of circum-stances, and most importantly by education.

A shortcut to looking over long time periods is to look at indica-tors of future performance: for example, performance in students' test scores, such as those administered under the OECD Pro-gramme for International Student Assessment (PISA) to 15-year-old students. Through these data, one can ask whether there are circumstances of the child, such as the education of his or her parents, the language spoken at home, or the number of books available, that significantly affect his or her performance in school. The answer to that question is that there are, and that the socio-economic conditions of households account for a significant part of the competencies gained at school by students (OECD, 2013b). Other studies show that childhood programs, the health of the mother, and exposure to adverse environmental conditions during pregnancy can have significant effects on how children develop (Currie, 2009).

Policy

While the available evidence shows that inequalities in child out-comes (e.g., among children with parents at different levels of educa-tion and income) are large and, in many cases, increasing over time, this evidence is limited in terms of both the outcomes considered and the age of the child. Were such evidence available, it might be possible to intervene earlier, and avoid more costly remedial inter-ventions at later ages. Mounting evidence on these inequalities, espe-cially for children born of parents in the bottom of the distribution, has led to a surge of interest around the world in early childhood education (Heckman and Masterov, 2004).

As individuals move through life, they experience a variety of shocks (sickness, layoffs, etc.). The ability to respond to such shocks—as well as the probability of experiencing such a shock, its depth, and duration—are, to a large extent, determined by circumstances. This is probably the main source of inequality of opportunity appearing during adult life. The availability of data on these circumstances would help in evaluating the role of social policies in neutralizing the long-run effects of such shocks.

While our discussion has focused on inequalities of opportunity in terms of income and wealth, just as important is the opportunity to live a long and healthy life. Especially in countries where there is inadequate public provision of health care services, a child born of poor parents faces a greater prospect of a shorter and a less healthy life. Health and economic outcomes are, of course, deeply interrelated, with low income contributing to, and resulting from, poor health. Just as there is intergenerational transmission of economic advantages and disadvantages, the same applies to health.

Gender is a key circumstance shaping outcome inequalities, and many of the indicators conventionally used to chart gender inequalities, such as earnings differentials, point to a progressive, albeit slow, reduction of these inequalities, at least in OECD countries. This conclusion is however less clear-cut when controlling for the many characteristics influencing earnings (e.g., education, job experience). Figure 3.3 (drawn from Chapter 5 by Bourguignon in the companion volume, itself sourced from Weichselbaumer and Winter-Ebmer, 2005) shows that when some of these other characteristics are controlled for, there is little or no reduction of women's earnings gap (the continuous line in Figure 3.3). In other words, a circumstance of birth—gender—remains a critical determinant of outcomes when controlling for observable aspects of effort such as education. There is no equality of opportunity, as the economic system treats differently a man and a woman with the same characteristics. This, in turn, implies that policies that are only aimed at raising women's participation in school and the labor market are failing to address enduring wage discrimination.

Figure 3.3. Gender Earnings Gap and Adjusted Earnings Gap in a Meta-analysis of the Literature

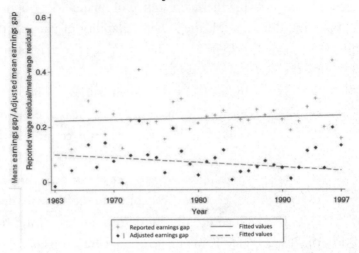

Source: Weichselbaumer, D. and R. Winter-Ebmer (2005), "A Meta-analysis of the international gender wage gap," *Journal of Economic Surveys*, Vol. 19(3), pp. 479–511.

Nothing is more important for our sense of a fair society than ensuring equality of opportunity, yet in no domain is the gap between the data we need and the data we have greater. Closing this gap will require persistent, concerted, and coordinated action: we need standardized data sets over long periods of time.

Subjective Well-Being

The objective of economic and social progress is to increase people's well-being. Who knows better than people themselves how well off they are and what most affects their own well-being? Money isn't everything in life, and just because an individual is richer doesn't mean he is happier or better off.

These ideas seem almost obvious, but they suggest an approach for looking "beyond GDP" to assess how well people and society are doing. Is GDP growth increasing the perceived (or what has come to be called *subjective*) well-being of most citizens? As obvious as it may seem, it is only recently that economists, working with psychologists, have attempted to pursue this approach to the assessment of economic performance and social progress. A major stimulus to this work, and to the inclusion of subjective well-being questions in official surveys, has been provided by the analysis in the 2009 Commission report and its recommendation to the National Statistical Offices to include such questions in their surveys. The Commission report highlighted the potential of this approach. Subjective well-being provides information that is not reflected in conventional economic statistics, although, conversely, conventional economic statistics may also provide information that is not captured by subjective well-being data.

In the words of Stone and Krueger in Chapter 7 in the companion volume: "Measures of subjective well-being . . . ask individuals to self-report ratings of aspects of their lives, including satisfaction with their life as a whole, their feelings at a particular moment, or the extent to which they feel that their lives have meaning or purpose. These measures focus on what people believe and report feeling, not their objective conditions."

A case in point that has attracted some attention was the sharp decline in life evaluation measures in several Arab countries in the years preceding the Arab Spring, despite strong GDP growth and improvements in health and education experienced in these countries (Figure 3.4). Other examples, quoted by Stone and Krueger in their chapter, are the findings that life evaluation is a stronger predictor of electoral results than conventional economic measures, and that the losses in average life-evaluation associated with a decline in GDP are twice as high as the gains from a GDP increase of similar size, a result that is consistent with standard results in behavioral economics on "loss aversion" (Kahneman and Tversky, 1984).

Figure 3.4. Trends in Subjective Well-Being in Egypt

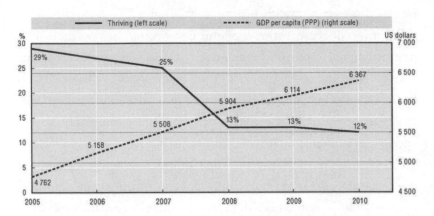

Note: Subjective well-being data are from the Gallup World Poll. GDP per capita estimates (at purchasing power parities) are from the IMF World Economic Outlook database.
Source: Reproduced from OECD (2013c), *OECD Guidelines on Measuring Subjective Well-Being*, OECD Publishing, Paris, http://dx.doi.org/10.1787/-en.

Since 2009, there has been enormous progress both in addressing technical problems and in the use of measures of subjective well-being. The report released in 2015 by the US National Academy of Sciences represents an important milestone (Stone and Mackie, 2015), while the OECD *Guidelines on Measuring Subjective Well-Being* have, since their release, been adopted by Statistical Offices in almost all OECD countries (OECD, 2013c).

Underlying the success of subjective well-being measures are several research findings. First, information obtained in this way is *replicable*, and the statistics produced have a high degree of reliability. Second, these measures themselves can, at least in part, be explained and the explanations make intuitive sense. For example, people who live in conflict zones, like Syria, report very low levels of subjective well-being; also, across countries, an increase in average income increases people's subjective well-being. As noted in the previous chapter, the Great Recession lowered people's subjective well-being in countries most affected by the crisis (OECD, 2015b), especially for those who had lost their jobs.

Explaining subjective well-being is not only of academic interest. It provides us with tools for enhancing individual and societal welfare. If being employed matters for people's subjective well-being, then this evidence should provide impetus for stronger responses to economic downturns, and perhaps even a justification for a government jobs program. This is even more true if economic insecurity adversely affects subjective well-being and if there are compounding effects, i.e., both unemployment and economic insecurity have a direct effect on subjective well-being, but the combination of the two may have impacts that are multiplicative rather than just additive. These measures in turn may help explain other variables of interest, though here research is still progressing, and we have to worry about causality. For example, as noted by Krueger and Stone, there is a positive correlation between people's health status and their subjective well-being, but it may be that low subjective well-being leads to negative health consequences, rather than the other way around, where negative health consequences lead to low subjective well-being. In reality, causality runs both ways. It will also be important in the future to assess the consequences of lower subjective well-being for trust and for people's view of how the political system functions.

Throughout this book and the companion volume, we have emphasized the interrelations among the various threads discussed in this chapter, and this is especially true for subjective well-being. Economic downturns affect insecurity, as we just noted, but economic insecurity also affects health, and health and insecurity both affect subjective well-being. Unemployment, or even the threat of unemployment, affects economic insecurity as well as subjective well-being. Recognizing these interrelations is important for at least two reasons. First, it helps us understand the multiple channels through which changes in policy may affect economic performance and societal well-being. And, second, in many cases, it helps us understand that there may be multiplier effects, not just the positive effects upon which we are focusing (e.g., the benefits of, say, expansionary fiscal policy on GDP) but indirect effects as well, through the reduction of economic insecurity, the increase in human capital, and the strengthening of wealth accumulation, all adding up to what we are really interested in, i.e., the impact of policy on people's lives.

Technical Issues

The 2009 Commission report argued that subjective well-being is in itself a multidimensional construct encompassing several different aspects, such as life evaluations, positive and negative experiences, and *eudaemonia* (having a sense of purpose in life). Each of these aspects requires its own metrics, and better understanding of its drivers.

Evaluative measures require a person to reflect upon and evaluate his or her life. Survey questions can be used to elicit people's summary evaluations of their current lives. Measures based on these questions also appear to be broadly consistent with people's choices, as people tend to make decisions based on their projected impact on their own life valuations, which can therefore be understood in terms of the economists' standard concept of "utility."

Experiential measures are different: they assess an individual's feelings, emotions, and states (happiness, sadness, pain) at a given moment. These measures are sensitive to the resiliency and the capacity of individuals to adapt.

Eudaemonia measures the extent to which a person believes that his or her life has meaning and purpose, and is also related to a person's psychological functioning.

These different metrics sometimes give different assessments of an individual's well-being. They are also affected by different variables and, in turn, have different implications for observed behavior. Understanding the differences is an area of ongoing research.

In most self-reporting, people are reflecting on past experiences, not on their subjective well-being at the moment. The two can differ, sometimes markedly. When parents are asked to respond to questions about the experiences of raising a young child *at the moment*, they often respond less positively than they do when asked years later. Both of these perspectives may reflect important and different aspects of well-being, but for many purposes, including for understanding decision making and certain other outcomes like health, it is the contemporaneous assessment that is especially relevant. To avoid some of the problems that arise as a result of these disparate subjective assessments, the collection of real-time or near-time data should be encouraged, especially for reporting of people's experiences and feelings. However, real-time data collection is expensive and sometimes impractical, so the standard has become the use of questions that ask about experiences in the past.

The order in which questions are asked—a standard methodological issue in all household surveys—is especially important for surveys that ask questions on subjective well-being, requiring careful consideration in survey design. There is also a problem of interpersonal comparability. Different groups may interpret the questions differently, or have in their mind different reference points. How can one know that an Italian who rates himself at 3 on a 0–10 point scale really has a lower level of subjective well-being than a Frenchman who ranks himself as 4? Problems of interpersonal comparability of this kind have long plagued welfare economics, the branch of economics centered on making judgments about the performance of economic systems. We currently lack the evidence needed to ascertain whether interpersonal differences in the use of a response scale are random (hence canceling out in large samples) or systematic across groups and countries. Researchers on subjective well-being have explored ways to address these interpersonal comparability problems (e.g., through vignettes—i.e., concrete examples of people and their behaviors on which survey participants offer an assessment that is then used to scale their own responses), while guidance on question wording, response format, survey mode, and context effects allows measurement errors to be managed and reduced. Research exploring the importance of cultural effects on people's responses to subjective well-being questions also indicates that these effects, while significant, explain only a small fraction of country-differences in life evaluation (Exton, Smith, and Vandendriessche, 2015). More generally, if one can't be sure about comparison of levels, *changes* can be meaningful. We can, in other terms, assess how changes in circumstances affect people's subjective well-being, as the discussion below illustrates.

Some Further Insights

A long-standing issue in research is the relationship between subjective well-being and income. Early "happiness" studies (Easterlin, 1974) suggested that, as countries reach a certain level of GDP per capita, their average subjective well-being (life evaluation) didn't increase. A great deal of effort has gone into explaining this "Easterlin paradox." For instance, if subjective well-being is related to one's *relative* position, then if everyone's income doubles, one's relative position will be unchanged, in which case subjective well-being would not change either. Recent studies have enhanced our understanding of the relationship between GDP and subjective well-being (Stevenson and Wolfers, 2012) but many aspects of the relationship remain unsettled. We know, for instance, that the shape and strength of the relationship depends on which aspect of subjective well-being (evaluative, experiential, eudaemonistic) is considered. At lower levels of income, the association between GDP and subjective well-being is positive whatever the specific aspect considered, while at higher levels of income evaluative well-being is positively associated with per capita GDP whereas experiential well-being is not (Kahneman and Deaton, 2010).

We also know that many other factors beyond income influence subjective well-being (Helliwell, Layard, and Sachs, 2018). Being employed, in better health, having stronger relationships, and just being connected with others are among the most important factors, with many other factors also identified in research. For instance, environmental conditions and (lack of) air pollution not surprisingly contribute to subjective well-being. There is also strong evidence of the importance of childhood experiences for people's subjective well-being as adults, and of the importance of people's resilience, i.e., their capacity to bounce back when confronting shocks. Childhood subjective well-being and children's emotional health are strong predictors of adult life satisfaction (Layard et al., 2014).

Subjective well-being studies have provided us insights into how people fare over their life. There are, of course, other indicators, such as depression and suicide, but these are indicators that might be viewed as capturing "extremes" in subjective well-being. As shown by Krueger and Stone in their chapter in the companion report, in most Western countries, there is a U-shaped pattern of life evaluations with respect to age, a pattern that does not hold for experiential well-being (which is often low for young people) and that is absent in poorer countries (Steptoe, Deaton, and Stone, 2015). This relationship holds across different birth-cohorts. This suggests that people's life priorities change as they age (away from income), implying that policies toward the elderly should focus on a range of aspects beyond income security in old age.

Differences in subjective well-being—for example, between individuals at different ages or in different circumstances—can also enrich distributional analysis. Elsewhere, in this and the companion volume, we speak of "inequalities." But perhaps the most important inequalities are those associated with subjective well-being. These should be more systematically measured and reported.

Further Research

Our earlier discussion (and, even more so, the chapter by Stone and Krueger) has already called attention to many areas where further research is needed. For instance, we noted that there are measures for different aspects of subjective well-being. It will be important to understand better their relationship with each other, the factors that affect each, and the consequences of each.

The *measurement* agenda is a comprehensive and interrelated one. We already noted the importance of subjective well-being as a mediating variable. As we get better measures of economic insecurity, for instance, we will be able to ascertain better how economic insecurity affects subjective well-being; and as we get better metrics of trust, we can ascertain better how subjective well-being affects trust, thus providing a more comprehensive perspective on the determinants of societal well-being.

While there has been great progress in collecting subjective well-being data, these are still far from adequate, particularly if we are to assess changes over time (such as might be associated with an economic downturn) or across countries. A low-cost way to increase data availability about subjective well-being is to add subjective well-being questions to existing surveys. We encourage National Statistical Offices to continue regular, frequent, and standardized collection of subjective well-being data based on the *OECD Guidelines*.

Economic Insecurity

In the late 1990s, the World Bank surveyed around 60,000 individuals living in poverty in 60 countries around the world in its project on *Voices of the Poor* (Deepa et al., 2000). The project asked poor people about what aspects of their lives presented the greatest hardship. Their answer, after initial comments about the obvious deprivation of income, was their sense of economic insecurity.

Concern about economic security grew during the financial crisis that erupted in 2008. Even those who had not yet lost their job realized that their jobs were at risk as the unemployment rate soared. More than 12 million people are estimated to have lost their jobs in OECD countries from the last quarter of 2008 to the first quarter of 2010, when the employment count reached its trough. Small businesses experienced large falls in sales, sufficient to push many to the brink of bankruptcy, and many went over the brink. Declining asset and housing wealth affected many people, especially those in or nearing retirement. Young people graduating from school worried whether they would be able to get a job, especially one commensurate with their education and talents, and in countries where tertiary education is often financed by student loans they worried about whether they would have sufficient income just to repay their debt.

The impact of the crisis on people's sense of economic insecurity may have been all the greater because, even before the crisis, large parts of society had faced growing insecurity due to changes in the economy, society, and policies. For instance, areas of the world confronting deindustrialization saw life prospects in decline. Without adequate systems of social protection, active labor market policies, and policies ensuring near-full employment, the result was high insecurity.

It is, accordingly, natural that the topic of economic security is nowadays a greater concern than at the time when the Commission report was published in 2009, not only for citizens, but also for economists and policy-makers.

As argued by Jacob Hacker in Chapter 8 of the companion volume, economic insecurity is a major aspect of people's well-being. One of the reasons that governments did not pay sufficient attention to it was that it was not adequately reflected in our standard statistics.

We focus here on economic security, but the boundary between economic security and other forms of security is hazy. Countries like the United States with inadequate systems of health care and disability insurance, forcing especially those with limited incomes to face high levels of health insecurity, have high levels of economic insecurity. A major determinant of personal bankruptcy in the United States is an extended period of illness or expensive health expenditures for some member of the family. In countries with high levels of physical insecurity, people also face the risk of serious losses of their assets from theft.

The Concept of Economic Insecurity

Hacker defines economic insecurity as "individuals' (or households') degree of vulnerability to economic loss." This broad definition includes three elements: (1) the probability of an adverse event (a *shock*); (2) the negative consequences from this shock (the *loss*); and (3) the kinds of protection to prevent or cover these losses (the *buffers*). All three elements are inherent in this definition: some probability of an adverse event; some negative economic consequence if this event occurs; and some set of protections (from formal insurance, to informal risk sharing, to self-insurance through savings and the like) that potentially offset or reduce the impact of the losses. All of these elements of economic security are crucial when it comes to the development of measures to capture overall economic insecurity.

Within this definition, one can also distinguish between "observed" (or objective) insecurity, where analysts use economic data to determine whether an individual or household is, in some sense, at risk of experiencing large reduction in, say, consumption (perhaps reflected in large proportions of those within a particular group experiencing such large reductions); and "perceived" (or subjective) insecurity, reflecting the sense of vulnerability felt by individuals. With measures of perceived insecurity, individuals themselves reveal their subjective response to their economic situation, whether through surveys, experiments, or some other revelation technique.

The Drivers of Growing Economic Insecurity

Even before the financial crisis, citizens and leaders in advanced democracies expressed concern that economic security was declining. In developing countries, governments grappled with new economic risks as people moved into wage labor, and the traditional risk-spreading role of the family declined. In both developed and developing countries, public concern centered on the changing character of the economy and society with, for instance, the fast-paced changes driven by globalization and technological advances, rising health care costs, and lower pension benefits (especially in relation to previous earnings) in many countries, and on the roles of governments, markets, and households in coping with the related economic risks.

Economic insecurity stems from the interaction of shocks, impacts, and buffers, with changes in any of the three potentially leading to higher economic insecurity. Changes in the structure of the economy or in economic policies can increase people's economic insecurity by increasing the probability of a negative shock or its impact or by reducing buffers available to respond to shocks. For instance, changes in family arrangements that increase the likelihood of living alone have reduced the protections provided by the family. Financial globalization, it was argued, would enable countries to better manage risks, borrowing in bad times and repaying in good; but in fact, for most countries (and for most individuals), it has also increased volatility and insecurity, with capital flows typically being pro- rather than counter-cyclical. Digitalization increases consumer choice and provides access to new services, but also fuels concerns about the effects of robotics and artificial intelligence in displacing jobs and entire occupations, increasing people's fear of losing their job and income.

The risks that can lead to economic losses are many, and stretch beyond the economic realm narrowly defined. While some of them are recognized by existing social security programs (e.g., unemployment, disability, illness, old age), others are often disregarded (as in the case of long-term care needs for the frail and elderly, of mental health problems, and of frequent shifts between low-paid work and unemployment) or addressed through programs originally devised for addressing risks that no longer exist (such as programs for war widows, which are used today in the United States to address the needs of single mothers).

Many reforms to social protection or health care introduced in recent years, pursued either to contain costs or to extend coverage, have reduced buffers available to people or shifted risks to those less capable of protecting themselves against them. As we discuss later, the weakening of social protection systems has had the collateral effect of increasing economic insecurity. In developing countries, the security provided by family support systems has typically weakened faster than countries have been able to provide public systems of social protection. Similarly, in advanced countries, the shift from defined benefit to defined contribution retirement systems has shifted risk from pension schemes to the elderly.

Even good systems of social protection do not fully offset the increase in economic insecurity associated with macro-economic volatility. This is especially so because individuals are more sensitive to an income loss of a given size than to a gain of the same amount ("loss aversion," as mentioned above). This evidence suggests that macro-economic policies should pay more attention to minimizing the bumps that the economy may face rather than just focusing on achieving the maximum GDP growth rate possible.

Increasing income inequality also increases economic insecurity: as the rungs of the ladder are further apart, slipping down a rung becomes more consequential. Labor market reforms aimed at increasing flexibility, while giving more discretion to the employer, may have increased workers' economic insecurity, except in those countries where unemployment benefits were raised and policies that helped workers find a new job quickly introduced.

Consequences

The consequences of economic insecurity can be severe, both economically and politically, both for individuals and for society as a whole. Economic insecurity is a source of stress and misery for people around the world. When individuals worry about the future, trying to figure out how various contingencies might affect them when they are just getting by as it is, they are less able to make good decisions, including about those elements that will affect their future well-being. There is not just a present cost of economic insecurity, but a future cost as well.

An increase in economic insecurity affects well-being and economic performance through many other channels. Autonomy at work is reduced by the fear of losing one's job. Job satisfaction falls and, with it, overall well-being. Growing economic insecurity and inadequate safety nets make people less willing to take risks, undermining economic growth and entrepreneurship.

Economic insecurity is conceptually different from poverty. It affects a much larger share of the population than poverty does. Those above the poverty level but at risk of falling into it might feel high economic insecurity. Because of its wider reach, a growing sense of economic insecurity is more likely to lead to shifts in political power than changes in poverty headcounts. Perhaps the increase of populist voting after the crisis would have been less of a surprise had the higher economic insecurity among large parts of the population prompted by the crisis and by ongoing structural and policy changes been recognized.

We noted earlier the increase in economic insecurity associated with deep downturns. But economic insecurity may also deepen and extend the downturn: individuals, worried about their future, may be hesitant to spend, just at a time when such spending could help spur recovery.

Market Failure and Policy

One might ask, if individuals value security in the same way they value the nutritional content of food, why isn't economic security reflected in market prices? Shouldn't the increased value of market products designed to reduce insecurity be reflected in higher GDP?

To some extent, this is already the case. The market does provide insurance that helps reduce economic insecurity, and the value of those products (the excess of the price of those products, i.e., of the benefits paid out, over their costs—the wages paid to those administering the system) is indeed included in GDP. But, due to informational asymmetries, transaction costs, and other market failures, insurance markets for many important contingencies do not exist.

Social protection systems were created to address these market failures and to reduce economic insecurity associated with unemployment, illness, disability, widowhood, and old age. But recent reforms have often shifted risks from governments to individuals, from firms to workers, and reduced the extent to which risks are "mutualized." Consider, for instance, the risks to economic security in old age. Before governments created public pensions (known as social security in the United States), the private market failed to provide annuities (i.e., assets paying someone a fixed amount of money for the rest of his or her life). Even today, transaction costs for annuities are large and, whether because of this or of information asymmetries or other market failures, buying a long-term bond is often more advantageous than buying an annuity. Yet, reforms of public pension systems have tended to put more reliance on the private sector. According to the EU's *Pension Adequacy Report*, the UK partial privatization of public pensions may have had the effect of reducing the projected pension benefits of men earning the average wage by 52% (European Commission, 2018, p. 114). More generally, the shift from defined benefit to defined contribution programs has shifted risk from corporations to individuals, even though the former are generally in a better position to bear and manage such risks.

There is an extensive literature on the fact that market failures are widespread in risk markets. Social insurance programs were created to make up for failures in insurance markets, and are often more efficient than private schemes, partly because they do not have advertising costs, partly because the private sector devotes large efforts at "cream skimming"—trying to make sure that they insure only those with the lowest risk. Some of these public institutions can be thought of as reflecting a social contract that arises from a democratic process. When these social contracts become more costly to maintain, policy reforms need to confront the risk that, as they try to make social protection systems financially sustainable, they may also increase the economic insecurity of groups of the population who have little capacity to bear it.

If our metrics do not capture the benefits that social insurance provides through greater economic security, there will be a tendency to focus on their costs, underestimating their benefits. The move toward a leaner welfare state is thus in part a consequence of not accounting properly for the benefits of the welfare state.

These benefits are, of course, greater than just the value of the increased individual security. If more secure individuals are more productive and/or are able to pursue higher-risk activities because of the presence of good social insurance, then society is better off, with some of the benefits of the increased productivity captured for the public benefit through taxation.

Concerns about moral hazard (adverse incentives) imply that it is not always desirable to provide complete insurance. The attack against social insurance, however, has gone beyond the level that can be so justified, especially today when so many people feel economically insecure. It is clear that we need to improve our metrics of economic insecurity and to assess policies for their impact on economic security, in addition to other goals.

Both globalization and technological change increase the likelihood of many of the risks mentioned above. Hence, their acceleration should be accompanied by higher and/or different (rather than lower) social protections, including systems that permit the portability of acquired rights across jobs and countries of residence, as well as investments in education and training to make people more resilient in the event of a negative shock. In all cases, however, it would be better to explicitly consider the effects of globalization and technological change on people's economic insecurity *ex ante*, rather than just coping with their effects *ex post*.

Metrics

There are two critical distinctions in designing metrics of economic insecurity. The first we referred to earlier: that between objective and subjective measures. The second distinction is between dashboards of economic security based on multiple measures, and integrated measures, which try to capture individual or household security in a single measure. For many reasons, dashboards are preferable to single indexes, which are less transparent and more sensitive to analysts' choice of components and weights.

One of the main challenges for researchers and Statistical Offices is to identify a limited set of measures of economic security that can be used in a broader dashboard of well-being indicators. These selected measures should generally be (1) broadly comparable across countries; (2) available over sufficient time periods to monitor changes; (3) closely linked to individuals' actual experience; and (4) capable of informing policy-makers as they seek to address economic security.

Surveys for assessing perceived economic security have the advantage of directly capturing individuals' perception of their personal and household economic conditions. However, they have two shortcomings: surveys have not been run for a significant time span, and questions differ among national surveys, thus hampering cross-country comparisons. Survey questions can be grouped in three categories: (1) general assessment of the economy (how one feels about the economy or the economic situation in the present or in the past); (2) perception of the buffers available to respondents (for example, the length of time respondents believe they could avoid economic hardship if faced with an adverse shock); and (3) expectations regarding future shocks (one's likely economic situation in the future or one's worry with regard to specific risks, such as job loss). All types of questions should be included in household surveys.

Objective measures try to quantify the shocks facing an individual (the probability of a shock and the depth and duration of the impacts) and the size of the buffers enabling individuals to cope with these shocks. One such measure, described by Jacob Hacker in his chapter in the accompanying volume, looks at the size of the population who experienced a large income loss (a fall in household-size-adjusted individual income from one year to the next of 25% or more). This measure, which relies on panel data following the same individual over time, is now available in a large number of industrialized countries; it shows large differences across OECD countries (Figure 3.5), with many countries experiencing increasing insecurity.[28] Other types of objective measures discussed by Hacker look at the key features (such as coverage and generosity) of the public programs that exist in various countries to address risks such as unemployment, disability, old age, and so on.

Figure 3.5. Average, Range, and Evolution of the Incidence of Large Income Losses Across Countries

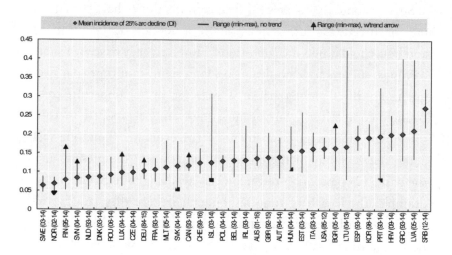

Note: Based on the following panel data collections: ECHP, EU-SILC, CPS, CNEF (BHPS, SOEP, HILDA, KLIPS, SHP, SLID). For each country, the period covered is indicated on the horizontal axis. Arc-changes, unlike percentage changes, treat gains and losses symmetrically (e.g., an income gain from USD 50 to USD 100 implies a 100% change but a 67% arc-change; while an income loss from USD 100 to USD 50 implies a 50% change but a 67% arc-change); they are bound between +2 and −2.
Source: Hacker, J. (2018), "Economic security," in Stiglitz, J.E., J.-P. Fitoussi, and M. Durand (eds.) (2018), For Good Measure: Advancing Research on Well-Being Metrics Beyond GDP, OECD Publishing, Paris. StatLink, http://dx.doi.org/10.1787/888933842147.

Further Research

Further work is required to select the best type of measure, to understand its properties, and to relate insecurity to other aspects of economic performance and individual well-being. The low availability of reliable and cross-nationally comparable data has been a crucial constraint on the development of improved measures of economic security. Three shortcomings of existing statistics stand out: the limited pool of long-term and cross-nationally comparable panel data about the income of various individuals; the weaknesses of most administrative data for tracing individuals over time; and the lack of regular questions about economic insecurity in conventional household surveys.

Measures of complex phenomena are necessarily imperfect, as is the measure of GDP, but that should not prevent us from going ahead. As Hacker observes, the implication of the remarkable advances in the measurement of economic insecurity is that governments should no longer ignore the effects of changes in economic structure and policy on economic insecurity. Policies and statistical practice cannot ignore something that is of first order importance for people and communities.

Sustainability

The importance of *sustainability* has been emphasized by the name of the goals that the world has set for itself for the coming decades: *Sustainable Development Goals*. GDP growth today that is at the expense of future generations is unacceptable. As we think about what we do today, we must bear in mind our legacy for the future. If we leave the world a worse place to live, then our own prosperity is at the expense of our descendants'. Economists and philosophers refer to this as *intergenerational equity*. People used to believe that future generations would automatically be better off than the current one, the only question being by how much. This assumption no longer holds.

Assessing sustainability requires determining if the current level of well-being can be maintained for future generations. By its very nature, sustainability involves the future and, as Yogi Berra quipped (paraphrasing Niels Bohr), "It's tough to make predictions, especially about the future." Its assessment involves many assumptions and normative choices. If (appropriately measured) wealth is increasing, then presumably society could do in the future whatever it does today, i.e., it can sustain its per capita well-being. But to assure that outcome, we need a *comprehensive measure* of wealth, and we need to use the right valuations. The Commission report in 2009 argued that measures of the sustainability of well-being are conceptually different from measures of *current* well-being, except to the extent that individuals' current well-being is adversely affected by anxieties over sustainability itself.[29] Well-being may be enhanced today by depleting some of the capital stocks essential for maintaining future production and future well-being.

Environmental, Economic, and Social Sustainability

The most immediate threat to sustainability is the *environment*. We live within a limited biosphere. Economists traditionally ignored these limitations and constructed models of economic growth *without end*. When, some half century ago, the Club of Rome started talking about *Limits to Growth* (Meadows et al., 1972), the response was a wave of technological optimism: we are innovative, the argument was, and whatever the Earth's limitations we can innovate around them. This techno-optimism has now been questioned, especially with the growing awareness of climate change brought about by the accumulation of greenhouse gases in the atmosphere, and natural scientists have quantified "safe operation boundaries" for several critical types of natural capital (Rockström et al., 2009). Of course, there may be a technological revolution, but right now, in the race between technology and humans' destruction of the single planet on which they live, technology is losing. We are on course for disruptive changes in our ecosystem, with temperatures and sea levels rising, and disease vectors and weather variability increasing—a host of changes that, at the very least, threaten to impose costs on future generations, which may well lower their standards of living, and significantly so. Major cities will be affected, and hundreds of millions, perhaps billions, of people relocated. The world faces countless environmental threats.

The 2008 crisis also showed that the economic system might itself not be sustainable. Much of the GDP growth that preceded the crisis was based on a bubble, and when the bubble burst, so did the seeming prosperity. Governments that thought that they were acting prudently (like Spain and Ireland) found that their spending was based on "bubble revenues." Families that thought they could get by with stagnating wages because their wealth was increasing as house prices soared, and that they could increase their debt, were brought down to earth. They had been living beyond their means, and promises of ever-rising standards of living were shown to be false. Standards of living in large swaths of advanced countries were seen to be little better than they were decades earlier.

In 2009, the Commission emphasized the importance of looking at sustainability in all of these dimensions. It was keenly aware that standard economic measures captured none of this, and it struggled with the question of what indicators would best reflect sustainability. The Commission arrived at a consensus that *if* markets worked well, one could form a comprehensive measure of the "capital" of the country, i.e., the value of the resources that one generation passes on to the next. This would include all forms of capital—physical/economic capital (buildings and machines), human capital (and knowledge capital), natural capital (environmental resources), and social capital (trust and connections with each other). If we leave more capital to our descendants than we inherited, then our descendants are likely to be better off, and their standards of living will be at least as good as that of the current generation. We say then that such growth is sustainable. This is the *capital approach* to sustainability.

The Commission, however, recognized that there were many problems with this approach, especially with its practical implementation. The first, and most obvious, is that markets for the future often don't work very well. There was a housing bubble because markets put an excessively high value on real estate. For fifty years, economists have studied why markets so often systematically get these prices wrong. In the case of natural resources, the market failure is even more obvious: we generally don't impose a price on carbon emitters or on biodiversity loss.[30]

The obvious failures of market pricing led the Commission to suggest that within the dashboard of indicators, there ought to be some physical metrics, such as the carbon footprint or the levels of concentration of carbon in the atmosphere.

In the narrower sphere of economics, some asset metrics also need to be introduced (see below). Unfortunately, in much public discourse, attention gets centered on gross debt, and especially public debt. Chapter 2 emphasized that this is an unbalanced perspective: no one looking at a firm would consider its debt without also looking at its assets. You need to consider the overall balance sheet. Partial information is dangerous: focusing on debt alone may lead governments to take actions (like cutting productive investments) that more than offset the increased value of liabilities, leaving the country worse off.

Other aspects of wealth, such as social and human capital, present even more formidable challenges for measurement. The HLEG, as we noted, decided to focus its attention on one aspect only, trust, a key part of social capital (see below).

As argued by De Smedt, Giovannini, and Radermacher, in Chapter 9 of the companion volume, another problem with the capital approach is that it may suggest a straightforward trade-off: one could make up for the deterioration of environmental capital simply by adding more economic (physical) capital. This reasoning led some economists to suggest that it would be better to do nothing about climate change today; we should simply set aside enough money (economic capital) so that, should climate change occur, we would have made future generations better off by leaving them more capital overall.

Even at the time of the Commission report's release, we cast doubt on that analysis. As a practical matter, the magnitude of the increased economic capital that would be required to offset the effects of climate change simply wouldn't be forthcoming. Any rational discourse had to take into account risk, recognizing that in the worst outcomes, when the magnitude and consequences of climate change were most severe, we would be least able to take the actions to offset those effects.

The work of the HLEG has highlighted these risks in several ways. First, it highlighted the concepts of resilience and vulnerability. Second, it focused on the complexity of the economic/social/environmental system as a whole. Complex systems are characterized by extensive nonlinearities and interactions, which make them hard to predict. Even simple complex systems can give rise to chaotic dynamics, with the system oscillating forever without any discernible patterns. Small changes in initial conditions or in the parameter values of the system can give rise to large changes in the dynamics of the system. This inherent uncertainty should make us particularly cautious as we approach major changes in the ecosystem, and the marked increases in atmospheric greenhouse gases represent such a large change. As the debates on climate change unfolded, we already saw several examples of this, many of which were not fully anticipated: as the tundra has defrosted, methane gases have been released, which have hastened its melting. As the polar ice cap melts, the Earth reflects back less energy, exacerbating global warming. There can be sudden reversals in patterns of ocean currents.

Analytically, price systems work only when the underlying technology is "well behaved"—that is, it exhibits familiar patterns of diminishing returns, as seen when one adds more and more labor and capital to land in agriculture. The early pioneers in mathematical economics (Arrow and Debreu, 1954) recognized this.[31] Unfortunately it was a lesson that practical followers of market economics lost sight of—a mistake that has become increasingly important as attention has centered on a host of violations of conventional assumptions of economic models, such as those associated with R&D, learning, bankruptcy, contagion, and so on (Stiglitz and Greenwald, 2016; Battiston et al., 2013). The fact that systems dynamics can be so sensitive to slight perturbations in initial conditions and parameter values means that, even if it were possible to find competitive prices that might prevail in the future, it would be extraordinarily difficult to be sure what those prices should be, with small errors in estimates of the relevant parameters resulting in large changes in prices (Roukny, Battiston, and Stiglitz, 2017).

Vulnerability and Resilience

As important as risks are, most earlier analyses paid insufficient attention to the uncertainties and variabilities. Just as the previous section focused on how risk gave rise to economic insecurity at the individual level, here we need to focus on the consequences of risk to the sustainability of systems. There are two related questions.

First, what is the risk of a negative shock to the economic or environmental system, in particular of a shock that might make the growth path unsustainable (in which case past living standards might not be attainable in the future)? For instance, there is uncertainty about the relationship between current levels of greenhouse gas emissions—the total stock of these gases in the atmosphere—and future levels resulting from climate change. As shown by *The Stern Review* (2006), while stabilizing concentrations of greenhouse gases at the level of 450 parts per million (the level targeted by the 2015 Paris Agreement) will most likely limit the increase in global temperature to 2 degrees Celsius, greenhouse gas concentrations at this level still imply an 18% risk of a temperature increase of 3 degrees, and a 4% risk of an increase of 4 degrees or more. The system may be more fragile and vulnerable than we currently think, so that, for a given level of greenhouse gases concentration in the atmosphere, the size of temperature increase (with all the attendant knock-on effects) could be much greater than in the baseline scenario.

Second, what is the resilience of the system, i.e., how strong are its capabilities of recovering, for instance, from a large shock?

We can think of quantifying, at least in principle, the vulnerability of the economic and environmental system—taking into account its resilience—by asking (analogously to how we measure the impact of inequality), *How much would a person or a society be willing to give up (in terms of their wealth) to eliminate this risk?* Similarly, we could measure the value of an improvement in the resilience of the system by ascertaining by how much the "vulnerability premium" is reduced as a result. Both types of measures, however, are likely to vary across individuals and countries. The question of how much society would pay to reduce vulnerability entails judgments about its welfare across generations. In turn, any reasonable assessment of the welfare of future generations—especially taking into account the risks of very adverse scenarios on climate change and recognizing that, in those contingencies, society would have limited capacity to deal with the impending disaster—implies that we are almost surely not investing enough to reduce vulnerability.

Metrics of Environmental and Human Capital

In Chapter 2 we discussed the particular difficulties in measuring capital (notably human capital), especially in the aftermath of a crisis. We noted there how a lack of underestimating about the impact on wealth (and thereby on sustainability) of the recession and of the accompanying austerity policies led governments to not take strong enough policies to stimulate the economy.

We also discussed some of the flawed measures used to assess economic sustainability (looking just at the government gross debt-to-GDP ratio) and how these too may have contributed to a weaker-than-desirable response to the downturn. As we noted earlier, even in the lead-up to the crisis, standard metrics may have given an impression that the economy was doing better than it really was, and not just because the government's revenues were artificially inflated as a result of capital gains associated with the bubble. Higher risks incurred by banks raised the spread between interest rates on loans and deposits, and thereby the measured output of financial intermediaries.[32]

Since the 2009 report, there has been significant progress in the availability of data on environmental sustainability. In 2012, the UN Statistical Commission—the guardian of official statistics—adopted as a statistical standard (the same status given to the System of National Accounts) a set of "core" economic and environmental accounts (the System of Environmental-Economic Accounting, or

SEEA). The SEEA provides a framework in which environmental statistics are fully integrated with national accounts, and thus offers a measurement framework for analyzing the interactions between the economy and the environment.[33]

The SEEA accounts cover flows of natural resources, products, and residuals entering in (as inputs) and exiting from (as waste) the economic system. These accounts (which include both flow and asset accounts, in both monetary and physical units) cover minerals and energy resources; land and soil resources; timber resources; and water and aquatic resources; as well as other biological resources (United Nations et al., 2014).[34] While these core accounts start from an economic perspective, a separate set of ecosystem accounts (whose status is recognized as "experimental") starts from the perspective of ecosystems,[35] looking at both the relation between ecosystems and human activities, and at the relation among ecosystems (for example, how wetlands depends on water flows from a contiguous river basin). While these are important developments, implementation of these accounts will spread over a long period, with different countries giving priority to different types of natural resources. So we still fall short of having adequate measures of the risks to the natural system, and having scientific consensus on where the planetary boundaries and tipping points are (Steffen et al., 2015).

As we take a closer look at each of the elements of "capital," the notion underlying sustainability, we note many unresolved measurement problems, both at the conceptual level and in implementation. Beyond the issues on measuring trust and social capital discussed below, there are also unresolved controversies over the best way of accounting for the depletion of natural resources, the degradation of the environment, and the loss of biodiversity. For instance, the discovery (or the confirmation of the existence) of an economically exploitable natural resource (adding to the level of "proven reserves") is treated in the national accounts as an addition to wealth, implying that if discoveries and depletion move in tandem, there is no reduction in capital. That would be the case if there were an infinite amount of natural resources and all that was needed was to discover them. What is scarce, in this view, is information about where the resources are, rather than the resources in themselves. A more realistic view, though, is that in the case of many nonproducible and nonrenewable resources, resources are finite, and when we consume those resources, our natural capital is being reduced even if this may be offset by discoveries.

The SEEA addresses this issue. While the System of National Accounts only includes mineral and energy resources that are economically exploitable given current prices and technology, the SEEA includes (at least in theory) all known mineral and energy resources, exploitable and not exploitable. Nonetheless, extending the boundary of mineral and energy assets in the accounts is more easily done in physical than in monetary terms. The valuation of mineral and energy deposits, especially those that are currently nonexploited because of market prices that are below extraction costs, poses considerable challenges to Statistical Offices.[36]

Human capital is another important asset for individuals and communities to maintain their well-being over time. An increase in human capital, and a decrease in the inequality of its distribution, can have great positive effects on the economy and on the well-being of society. It enhances future productivity and the ability to innovate. People with higher education live longer; have higher earnings and accumulated wealth, better health conditions, denser networks of connections; and are more active citizens. While well-being, both now and in the future, is enhanced when human capital increases, people's skills and competencies decay when they are not used (e.g., in the workplace). Market and individual decisions may also lead to under-provision of human capital when the full range of its benefits is not fully recognized or doesn't accrue to the person or firm investing in it, or when there are capital constraints limiting the resources that an individual with limited means has to invest in himself.

The problem is that there is no fully satisfactory way of measuring human capital. One approach focuses on "costs" (like the costs of constructing physical capital). But physical capital goods are bought and sold in relatively competitive markets, so that the price of a machine reflects, in some sense, its underlying "value." Human capital is generated by formal education, most of which is publicly provided, but also by work experience and upbringing: in none of these cases do we have a good mechanism for assessing the value of the asset that has been acquired. Another approach looks at the "income generated," say by education and work experience, over the working life of each person. But this has at least two problems. First, it is impossible to identify with any precision how much of the income generated is a result of capital investment and of the individual's own efforts. It may be that individuals with more education, for instance, work harder, in which case some of the increased income associated with higher education is wrongly attributed to human capital, exaggerating the estimates of its magnitude and importance. Second, it suggests that the only value of human capital is to produce more goods and services. In this approach, when a person retires, he or she has no more human capital left. This is obviously wrong. Even then, human capital continues to yield dividends in terms of higher well-being.

While both of the approaches to human capital measurement described above aim to derive a monetary value of the stock of human capital, a more practical approach is the one used by the OECD to measure the key cognitive and workplace skills needed by adults to prosper in society, similar to that used to measure the skills and competencies of 15-year-old students. The OECD Survey of Adult Skills has so far been conducted in 40 countries, with second cycles starting in 2019. Physical measures of this type need to be continued in the future, and extended to more countries and to more types of (noncognitive) skills.

Social Capital and Trust

Previous sections have outlined aspects of economic performance that have typically been given short shrift in policy discussions, and suggested that one of the reasons for this is that they are inadequately reflected in our standard measures of economic performance, such as GDP and social progress.

Here we consider one area that has only recently moved into the purview of economic discourse: social capital in general and trust in particular. The Commission report in 2009 recognized the importance of social capital, the glue that holds society together, noting the importance of social ties within the community to individual and societal well-being. The extent of connectedness with other members of society varies widely between individuals, with people with more connections having advantages over others.[37] An important source of inequalities of opportunity is the unequal distribution of social capital.

Social capital allows contracts to be honored without resorting to courts. If every contract had to be enforced through the courts, the market system could not function.

Indeed, most economic relations are not based on contracts but on generalized trust. Traditionally, trust has been recognized as a fundamental factor in the history of finance and financial transactions. There is now a well-developed literature on social capital. Some of this is formalized through game theory, showing that it is rational, in repeated games, for people to act in a cooperative and trustworthy way (Dasgupta and Serageldin, 2000). More recently, a small literature has used insights from sociology and cultural psychology to explain trustworthy and cooperative behavior—for instance, to explain the success of micro-credit lending in Bangladesh and its failures in India (Haldar and Stiglitz, 2016).

The HLEG decided to focus its attention on one aspect of social capital, albeit a very important one—*trust*. Yann Algan, in Chapter 10 of the companion volume, defines trust as "a person's belief that another person or institution will act consistently with their expectations of positive behaviour." What makes the concept of trust so useful is: (1) there are a variety of relatively consistent ways by which it can be measured; (2) variations in levels of trust can be explained in ways that correspond to theory and common sense; and (3) trust metrics can be shown to be related to other measures of economic performance and individual well-being. Given the importance of trust, policy-makers should pay more attention to it, and to how their policies affect it.

The 2008 crisis reduced not just economic security but also trust. This was especially so because of the widespread perception of the unfairness in the manner in which the crisis was handled, as we showed in Chapter 2. The loss of people's trust (both in others and in institutions) is likely to be a long-lasting legacy of the crisis. This loss was predictable, given what we know about the determinants of trust.

We should think of trust as an asset, as a key part of social capital. Trust takes time to build but can dissipate quickly when people perceive that others did not behave in a trustworthy way. There are thus important hysteresis effects, i.e., long lasting impacts of past actions on present or future circumstances and behaviors.

There are many different forms of trust. A key distinction is that between trust among individuals (interpersonal trust) and trust in institutions (institutional trust). Similarly, within a given society, there can be trust in some institutions and not in others; trust among people you know personally but not among strangers (generalized trust). While trust in others and trust in institutions are different, they are also related. When institutions are dysfunctional and the rules of the game are perceived as unfair, they lower people's willingness to cooperate with each other, creating a "society of mistrust" (Coyle, 2013). It then becomes more difficult to implement policies for the common good, which helps create the conditions for populism and can even put democracy at risk (Inglehart and Norris, 2016).

Typically, trust diminishes the more distant the relationship or the institution is, as we go from "local" to "national" or "global," from families to clans to strangers. While each aspect of trust has its own determinants, causes, and consequences, some general patterns are discussed briefly below.

Metrics

Good measures of trust have been lacking, and this has contributed to policy-makers' failure to focus adequately on trust. Existing measures of trust in institutions are typically based on small-scale unofficial surveys that use a single question conflating different aspects of trust, for instance trust in different institutions, and provide only limited evidence of changes over time. Existing measures of trust in others have similar limits. Better understanding of trust and its drivers calls for better metrics.

Despite these limits, existing measures show huge cross-country differences in levels of trust in others (Figure 3.6), differences in trust between different institutions in the same country, and a downward trend in many countries (e.g., the United States, other English-speaking countries, and the European countries most affected by the crisis).

Figure 3.6. Trust in Others Around the World

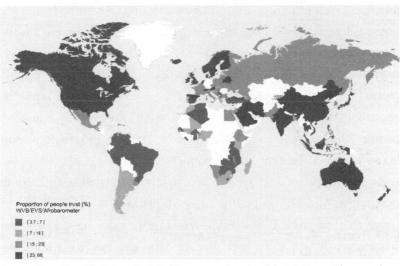

Source: Algan, Y. and P. Cahuc (2014), "Trust, growth and well-being: New evidence and policy implications," in Aghion, P. and S. Durlauf (eds.), *Handbook of Economic Growth*, Vol. 2, Elsevier/North-Holland, Amsterdam, pp. 49 120.

Trust is usually measured through answers to survey questions. Generalized trust, by which is meant trust in strangers, is evaluated in the World Values Survey through the question: "Generally speaking, would you say that most people can be trusted, or that you can't be too careful when dealing with others?" Trust is equal to 1 if the respondent answers: "Most people can be trusted" and 0 otherwise. Generalized trust is positively correlated with a range of positive phenomena: GDP per capita, subjective well-being, total factor productivity, financial development, co-operative relations between workers and management, quality of the legal system, and so on. Studies have shown enormous differences in trust not just across countries but also across regions of the same country (Putnam, Leonardi, and Nanetti, 1993) and across states in federal countries (Putnam, 2000).

Countries with higher levels of trust tend to have higher per capita income. (This is a correlation, not a causation. As we have already noted, there may be a two-way relationship, with greater trust leading to higher GDP, and a higher GDP leading to behaviors that stimulate trust, as well as other factors that may influence both trust and GDP.) Both generalized trust and trust in institutions are higher among higher-income groups and among more highly educated people. They are lower among unemployed people and single-person households with one or more dependent child.

As one might expect, trust is negatively correlated with income inequality. And rising income inequality has also been related to lower trust in institutions. High-trusting societies have lower levels of income inequality, measured by Gini coefficients, while low-trusting societies show typically higher levels of income inequality. Trust is undermined by things that run against people's sense of fairness. Since, at least in many countries, there is a general sense that income is inequitably distributed, it is not a surprise that economic equality is consistently identified as one of the strongest predictors of generalized trust, and that countries with highest levels of trust rank highest on economic equality (e.g., Nordic countries, the Netherlands, Canada; OECD, 2018a).

The adverse impacts on trust are among the "hidden costs" of inequality, which deepen fault lines in societies. It is undoubtedly one of the reasons behind the argument that income inequality has adverse effects on economic performance. Societies pay a high price for inequality, including through a loss of trust in each other and in institutions (Stiglitz, 2012a).

While the patterns described here hold true within and across the majority of OECD countries, it is important to study the drivers of trust in the context of countries' specific circumstances.

The Role of Trust in Our Economy and
the Consequences of a Lack of Trust

A growing literature has traced the growth of modern capitalism to trust (Greif, 1993, 1994). The modern financial system, arguably, would not have arisen without the high levels of trust that existed in the different Italian city-states, such as Florence.

For reasons that have been well described by Arrow (1972), trust matters a great deal in a market economy. It makes it unnecessary for market participants to engage in the impossible task of attempting to write contracts covering all types of future contingencies, and thus it improves the functioning of the economy. Arrow's intuition was straightforward. In the absence of informal rules like trusting behavior, markets are missing, gains from economic exchanges are lost, and resources are misallocated. In that respect, trust and the informal rules shaping co-operation can explain differences in economic development.

Responses to survey-based questions on trust are good predictors of macro-economic outcomes, but there is very little understanding of the micro-economic mechanisms involved, save the Arrow analysis.

Not surprisingly, trust is related to subjective well-being. For instance, cooperative social relationships with others, which are facilitated by trust and give rise to trust, affect people's health and happiness above and beyond the monetary gains derived from cooperation.

A lack of trust also has political consequences. Growing economic insecurity and higher unemployment lower trust in political institutions and this in turn leads to higher voting for populist parties. Trust is also rooted in places and closely knit communities whose members behave in a trustworthy manner toward other members of the same community (taking into account the well-being of others). Diversity, if not supported by integration policies, may erode this sense of communal trust and, more broadly, support for redistributive policies.

In turn, low trust in institutions leads to fewer people voting (this is especially true among the less educated and those with lower income)[38] or participating in policy in other forms. The growing gulf in the occupational background and economic circumstances between voters and their elected representatives also breeds mistrust. In a sample of OECD countries, manual workers and people in other elementary occupations make up 44% of the voting-age population, but only around 10% of the elected members of parliament (OECD, 2017a). In the United States, the median net worth of members of Congress was above $1 million in 2013, while the median net worth of American households was around $60,000 (Sitaraman, 2017). One implication is that less than 30% of all people in OECD countries feel that they have a say in what the government does.[39] The 2009 Commission report emphasized the importance of "political voice" for well-functioning democracies and for people's well-being. Judging from the current wave of populist votes in many developed countries, this is an area where we seem to be moving backward rather than forward.[40,41]

Policy

As trust plays a key role in explaining economic and social outcomes, it is urgent to identify the institutions and policies needed for it to develop. In particular, policy-makers need to pay attention to those actions that might erode it.

Actions and processes that are *perceived* to be "unfair" (for instance, in how people are treated in the processes by which decisions get made) undermine trust. In the United States, as we noted, the seemingly favorable treatment given to bankers, relative to that given to homeowners, undermined trust in government. So too in Europe, where the austerity measures imposed on crisis countries— with particularly adverse effects on the poor—were widely perceived as unfair, undermining trust in the key European institutions. At a minimum, governments engaged in policies that are so perceived have a duty to do a better job in persuading citizens that there is an underlying "just" rationale for the policies.[42]

More generally, measures of people's trust in various institutions, its causes and consequences, provide a point of entry for developing metrics of "how government functions" from the perspective of the people they serve. This is an important area for future statistical work. There are some obvious candidates for important determinants: when citizens' preferences do not get reflected in legislations, it undermines trust that the institutions are acting in any way consonant with democracy. Likewise, actions that limit democratic participation and enhance the influence of money should be expected to undermine trust in democratic institutions. These are all empirical questions that can be tested, with results that might shape a "trust building" agenda.

There has only been limited progress in identifying policies that most effectively promote trust. As shown by Algan in his chapter, the evidence that exists is mainly limited to the importance of education, including early interventions, with a focus on social (noncognitive) skills and teaching methods.[43] If this is so, it implies that we need to routinely measure those noncognitive skills that have an impact on trust through instruments like PISA and the Programme for the International Assessment of Adult Competencies (the OECD Survey of Adult Skills).

Further Work

We need to improve existing measures of trust. As we noted, trust metrics (either trust in others or trust in institutions) are typically derived from household surveys, but most evidence stems from non-official surveys with small and nonrepresentative samples that do not allow for seeing which parts of the population face the largest trust deficits. Advances in experimental economics and psychology have made it possible to verify correlations between trust as reported by respondents in surveys, and trust and other cooperative norms observed in laboratory experiments. The results suggest that survey measures, especially those of generalized trust, produce valid measures. In the future, it will be important to include these questions in the routine, large-scale data collection activities of National Statistical Offices. *The OECD Guidelines on Measuring Trust* (OECD, 2017b) provides information on various facets of statistical quality of existing trust measures, as well as practical recommendations on the type of questions that could be included in official statistics.

At the same time, efforts should continue to extend the complementary measures of trust that lab experiments can offer using representative population samples. Yann Algan describes in his chapter how these types of measures are already being implemented by researchers, as in the case of the Trustlab project, jointly managed by the OECD and Sciences-Po, Paris. Evidence from Trustlab can be used to assess the statistical quality of survey data (with evidence showing that people who report high trust in surveys also display more trusting behaviors in experimental games) but also to investigate what the key drivers of trust are. Results from Trustlab indicate that government integrity, its responsiveness, its openness, and the access it offers to quality services are the most important determinants of people's trust in government (Murtin et al., 2018). The same tools could also be used to explore other aspects of people's behaviors, such as discounting of future benefits, aversion to risks and uncertainties, and how (perceived) inequalities shape behaviors. But we also need stronger evidence that the ways people behave in games and experiments is a good guide to how they behave in real-life situations.

While research on the causes and consequences of trust is still in its infancy, it is proving to be a rich field of endeavor, with promising insights into our understandings of economic performance and social progress. This is especially important in the context of concerns about "fake news" and of the decline in trust in the media observed in many countries. There are profound consequences for any society if the sources of information cannot be trusted. The ability to have a rational discussion about alternative policies is undermined when there is no minimal agreement about what the "facts" are.

Earlier in this chapter, we identified several correlates of trust. But, to date, we still have an imperfect understanding of causality, and indeed, causality may often run in both directions. A lack of trust in public institutions may hamper their ability to engage in redistribution because there may be a fear that redistribution will go the wrong way, i.e., from the poor to the rich. But high levels of inequality, especially when they cannot be justified, also undermine trust in institutions. Similarly, a well-functioning legal system may enhance trust, while a lack of trust may lead to an overly rule-bounded legal system in which, in the process of following detailed rules, miscarriages of justice may end up undermining trust.

Because trust plays such an important role in economic and social performance, it is urgent to identify the institutions and public policies that will foster its growth. Developing better metrics would enable us to measure our successes in these endeavors.

Conclusions

All the areas discussed above will require greater research and better data in the years to come. Even for those areas that already feature prominently in ongoing statistical collection—such as vertical inequalities in household economic resources—there are important methodological challenges that stand in the way of adequately capturing underlying realities. Other areas—such as subjective well-being and environmental accounting—have only recently started to be covered by Statistical Offices, and measurement initiatives will need to be strengthened to extend the evidence base needed to improve the quality of these statistics. Other areas yet—such as economic insecurity, inequality of opportunity, trust, and resilience—currently lack a foundation in countries' statistical system. Greater investment is needed in all these areas, as the arguable lack of more-adequate metrics contributed to inadequate policy decisions.

4.

Country-Experiences with Using Well-Being Indicators to Steer Policies

This chapter evaluates differences that arise from approaching policy through a well-being lens. It describes the different ways in which well-being indicators could be used in the different stages of the policy cycle, from identifying priorities for action, to assessing the pros and cons of different strategies to achieve policy goals, allocate the resources (budgetary, human, political) needed to implement the selected strategy, monitor interventions in real time as they are implemented, and assess the results achieved and take decisions on how to change policies in the future. The chapter argues that a broad framework encompassing the most important dimensions of people's lives—paying attention not just to average outcomes but to how policies affect each segment of society, and giving a balanced consideration to well-being today and tomorrow, both domestically and in other parts of the world—holds the promise of delivering better results and bridging the divide that separates policy-makers and ordinary people today.

Introduction

As shown in the Annex of this book, the development of better indicators of economic performance and social progress has played an important role in developing a shared evidence-based understanding of what makes for better lives.[1] However, while broadening and improving metrics is needed to better assess countries' performance and the problems that may lay ahead, they do not, in themselves, lead to a change in the setting and framing of policy. In all countries, there is always the risk that the newly developed indicators become "just another report," rather than leading to a new approach to policy-making. Many of the well-being indicators included in the dashboards adopted by countries are already well-established, and they do play a role in orienting policies (e.g., unemployment). However, beyond the fact that, as argued in previous chapters, many such indicators still require improvement to help avoid some of the policy mistakes of the past, what is also important is that institutional mechanisms are in place to foster the use of these indicators by governments when taking decisions.

This chapter asks, What is different when policy is approached through a well-being lens?

Using Well-Being Indicators in Policy-Making

The sidebar titled "Stages in the Policy Cycle at Which Well-Being Indicators and Evidence Can Be Used," describes the different ways in which well-being indicators could be used in the different stages in the policy cycle, from identifying priorities for action, to assessing the pros and cons of different strategies to achieve policy goals, allocate the resources (budgetary, human, political) needed to implement the selected strategy, monitor interventions in real time as they are implemented, and, finally, assess the results achieved and take decisions on how to change policies in the future (Figure 4.1). The argument there is that a broad framework—encompassing the most important dimensions of people's lives—paying attention not just to average outcomes but to how policies affect each segment of society, and giving a balanced consideration to well-being today and tomorrow, domestically and in other parts of the world—holds the promise of delivering better results and bridging the divide that separates policy-makers and ordinary people today.

Using well-being metrics in a policy context can deliver many advantages. These include:

- *Providing a more complete picture of people's conditions in any given jurisdiction* (e.g., a country, region, or city) and drawing attention to outcomes that matter to people's lives but are not routinely considered in policy analysis simply because of a lack of suitable metrics. In a sense, this was where the "Beyond GDP" agenda began; as we noted, GDP simply did not capture key aspects of people's conditions.
- *Supporting the strategic alignment of outcomes across government departments.* Throughout the policy cycle, co-operation and cohesion across government is essential. Government agencies often operate in silos, focusing on the resources and outputs for which they are directly responsible (housing, health, education, employment, etc.) and without reference to the wider impacts of their actions. For example, crime and justice agencies will focus on the direct impacts of their actions in reducing crime and enforcing safety measures, despite the fact that spillovers from other policy areas and society-wide patterns (such as poverty, limited access to affordable housing, or lack of

public health and education services) may be large. Policy spillovers also operate in the other direction, with personal safety as a major determinant of outcomes in other policy areas, e.g., as a driver of education outcomes and social connections. Similar spillovers occur in *all* policy areas. By identifying the range of outcomes to be considered by all policies, frameworks for measuring people's well-being can promote consistency across government and provide a common language for agencies to discuss these impacts. Additionally, a multidimensional well-being framework (i.e., a framework that encompasses the range of aspects that matter to people's lives) can generate positive interactions between government agencies, pushing them to coordinate their actions and programs to achieve a higher-level objective and helping them to do so. These frameworks can also assist in clarifying responsibilities across and within different levels of government and different groups of stakeholders, increasing coordination among policies.

- *Highlighting the diversity of people's experiences through more granular data.* In contrast to many aggregate measures which focus on the performance of the economic system as a whole, metrics informing on outcomes at the individual and household level enable us to focus on inequalities, pockets of deprivation and vulnerability, and/or on groups whose outcomes are failing to keep pace with country-wide developments. The notions of "inclusive growth" at the OECD or of "shared prosperity" at the World Bank are attempts to put more focus on assessing how the benefits of economic growth are distributed.

- *Considering both well-being outcomes today and resources for tomorrow.* As we highlighted in the previous chapter, a key limit of GDP is that it doesn't take sustainability into account, either in terms of whether economic growth is itself sustainable over time or whether growth is being achieved with environmental and social costs that offset part (or most) of its economic benefits. The broad coverage (i.e., economic, environmental, and social) of well-being measures is here a key advantage. In addition, most approaches to measuring well-being include forward-looking elements, such as indicators of natural, human, social, and economic capital stocks that will support well-being in the future (although, as seen above, much progress still remains in measuring these capitals). This balances out the short-term focus of most policy decisions (on the "here and now") and enables governments to examine whether progress on well-being today is being achieved at the expense of depleting stocks of resources for future generations ("later") or in other countries ("elsewhere").[2]

• *Promoting more comprehensive evaluations of the impact of specific policies on people's lives.* Encouraging different government departments to consider the wide range of well-being outcomes and impacts of their programs has the potential to help policy-makers identify impacts of programs, and articulate trade-offs and spillovers more explicitly and transparently. Accountability for results is fundamental to efficient and effective governance. It is the ultimate rationale for evaluating policy interventions *ex post*, and is an important input into strategic priority setting. Well-being frameworks can form the basis for the accountability procedures of government agencies. In defining the set of desired outcomes expected from policy interventions through a range of indicators relating to people's well-being, *ex post* policy evaluation can increase accountability for a wider range of outcomes than previously considered. Agreement on the dimensions and indicators of people's well-being can also streamline external accountability measures, such as those exercised through parliamentary oversight and audit agencies and by civil society, creating a common language and a consensus on the types of benefits expected from various policies and programs.

- *Fostering public debate.* Regular reporting, monitoring, and evaluation using well-being metrics allows a country-wide discussion, based on a common concept of what makes for a good life, between all stakeholders, from politicians to civil society, businesses, and ordinary citizens.

Mechanisms for Integrating Well-Being Indicators in Policy Decision Making

Routine reporting of well-being statistics can, in itself, help to highlight issues and inform policy decisions in the agenda-setting phase of the policy cycle. Simply making data on levels, inequalities, and trends in well-being available to a wide range of stakeholders (i.e., civil society, politicians, business, and the media) can shift opinion, inform debate, and influence priority-setting. For example, availability of credible data on students' skills, based on standardized assessment of their competencies through PISA, has had a huge impact in shifting the focus of educational policies beyond attendance and graduation to what is actually learned by students in schools.

Nevertheless, to unleash some of the potential benefits of well-being metrics outlined above, it is necessary to go beyond simply *making indicators available* to wide audiences. For example, integrating well-being metrics in policy formulation and evaluation requires a conscious decision on the part of those performing or commissioning this research and analysis, as well as a demand from decision makers for a more comprehensive evidence base on which to draw. It also requires an established set of tools, models, and techniques recognized across the analyst profession within governments (such as the methods set out in the United Kingdom Treasury's *Green Book: Appraisal and Evaluation in Central Government* [HM Treasury, 2018], to evaluate the costs and benefits, monetary and nonmonetary, of all government programs).

Several OECD countries have developed formal and structured mechanisms to ensure that well-being or "Beyond GDP" indicators are integrated into their policy processes. These mechanisms can target a specific stage of the policy cycle depicted in Figure 4.1 or encompass several. These specific mechanisms or procedures provide a good point of entry for a "Beyond GDP" analysis, for they allow for ascertaining whether they give adequate weight or attention to the various other dimensions of well-being beyond aggregate economic output. For instance, many countries require a cost-benefit analysis, say, for energy programs, with the impacts in the future discounted. Current procedures used in many countries effectively imply that negligible weight is given to the impacts of climate change 40 years from now; in short, the procedures do not ensure sustainability.

Table 4.1 provides an overview of such experiences in 10 countries that have adopted well-being policy frameworks, identifying the leading agency and the stage of the policy cycle addressed by the mechanism put in place (see Exton and Shinwell [2018], which describes the settings in which the policy mechanisms and frameworks were developed in these countries). From these case studies, it is possible to identify some common themes, differences, and challenges that arise when implementing well-being frameworks into policy settings. Common themes relate to the measurement framework itself, the process used to reach consensus on its features, and the political context of each country.

STAGES IN THE POLICY CYCLE AT WHICH WELL-BEING INDICATORS AND EVIDENCE CAN BE USED

One way to characterize the various opportunities for metrics to influence policy decisions is to consider the different stages of the policy cycle (Figure 4.1). Building on the various approaches described in the literature (e.g., Jann et al., 2006; Cairney, 2013), it is possible to distinguish among the following stages:

1. *Priority/agenda setting.* Based on a strategic analysis of the current situation, including trends over time and inequalities, a strategic review of policy goals may lead to identifying areas that require government intervention, followed by prioritization and agenda setting. This stage typically involves national government or parliament and national planning agencies, as well as citizens, often acting through civil society, bringing to the attention of policymakers perceived deficiencies in outcomes and processes.

2. *Policy formulation (ex ante).* This stage includes the investigation of policy options, the evaluation of their costs, benefits, and feasibility, and finally the selection of relevant policy instruments and levers. This stage usually involves a national planning agency and the government agencies responsible for designing and delivering the policy interventions, allocating financial resources among government agencies, and making decisions on budgeting.

3. *Implementation.* This phase involves executing programs and policy interventions by the government agencies responsible for implementation, and providing them with the necessary resources, in accordance with prioritization and policy formulation.

4. *Monitoring.* A prerequisite for evaluating policy impacts

is that the policy interventions are monitored, both during and after implementation. Monitoring involves taking stock of the inputs used for the policy intervention, the outputs generated, and the outcomes observed; a comprehensive evaluation can also benefit from monitoring the counterfactuals of the policy intervention. At this stage, the national planning agency and the government agency implementing the policy, as well as external stakeholders, may be involved to monitor the impacts of policy interventions.

5. *Evaluation (ex post).* This stage requires assessing the results of the policy intervention in view of its goals, and deciding on either termination or continuation. This stage of policy-making can involve the national planning agency and the various potential stakeholders as well as central auditors' offices.

Figure 4.1. The Policy Cycle

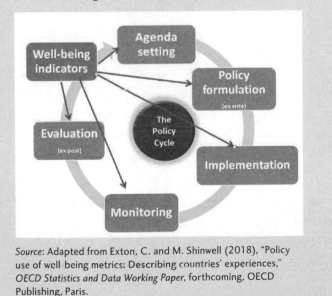

Source: Adapted from Exton, C. and M. Shinwell (2018), "Policy use of well-being metrics: Describing countries' experiences," *OECD Statistics and Data Working Paper,* forthcoming, OECD Publishing, Paris.

Selected Countries' Experiences with Implementing Well-Being Indicators in the Policy Cycle

As noted earlier, in some countries well-being indicators were not specifically developed with policy use in mind. In others, however, the process started with a paradigm shift at the policy level, aiming to expand what is considered important to improve people's lives. In Ecuador, for example, the concept of *buen vivir* (good living) was embedded in the country's new constitution, put in place in 2008. Somewhat similarly, in Scotland, well-being indicators were given a central role through their integration into a national performance framework and monitoring procedures. The stages of the policy cycle in which indicators are used differ as well. Well-being indicators are mostly used at the policy formulation stage (e.g., in New Zealand and Ecuador) or at the evaluation stage. In France, Italy, and Sweden, indicators are more commonly used at the agenda-setting stage, with parliamentary reporting based on these indicators at the start of the budget process (see Table 4.1). These are just selected examples. Other countries, such as Bhutan, Mexico, Colombia, Slovenia, and Costa Rica, have also developed well-being frameworks and indicators to guide their policies.

The number and type of indicators used in policy settings varies significantly across countries. In Sweden, Italy, and France, where policy use is mainly through reporting to parliament, the number of indicators is very limited (from 6/10 in France, to 12 in Italy and 15 in Sweden) in order to facilitate parliamentary discussion. At the other extreme, in New Zealand and the United Kingdom a very wide variety of indicators are provided by the National Statistical Office and used for cost-benefit analysis or *ex post* evaluation of a range of policy interventions (in the United Kingdom, through the What Works Centre for Wellbeing)[3] or for *ex ante* policy design

Table 4.1. Mechanisms and Frameworks for Integrating Well-Being Metrics into Policy-Making in Selected Countries

Country	Mechanism	Leading agency	Short description	Stop of the policy cycle targeted
Australia	Well-being framework	Treasury	A well-being (Living Standards) framework was developed in 2004 by the Treasury to underpin analysis and advice across the areas under its responsibility. The framework includes 5 well-being elements (consumption possibilities, their distribution, the risk borne by individuals and society, the complexity of choices, and the freedom and opportunity enjoyed by people). In 2016 the Treasury Living Standards framework was updated, focusing on the budget, productivity, and globalization.	Policy formulation, policy evaluation
Ecuador	- Constitution - Nat. Development Plan - Buen Vivir Secretariat	Government	The concept of *buen vivir* was integrated in the Ecuadorian constitution in 2008. In June 2013, former President Rafael Correa created the "Buen Vivir Secretariat" as a new Ministry within the national government. A key mechanism is the National Development Plan, which lays out the national strategy for Buen Vivir every four years.	Agenda-setting, policy formulation, policy evaluation
France	Budget law, drawing on New Indicators of Wealth	France Strategy and the Economic, Social and Environmental Council (EESC)	Approved in April 2015, law 411 requires the Government to submit an annual report to Parliament on progress on 10 new indicators reflecting the country's economic, social, and environmental situation. The report, which should include an assessment of the impact of the main reforms envisaged on these indicators, can be debated in Parliament upon request by the government.	Agenda-setting, policy formulation, policy evaluation
Italy	Budget law, drawing on the BES ("equitable and sustainable well-being") framework	Ministry of Economics and Finance	Building on the National Statistical Institute's BES framework, a law approved in 2016 stipulated a narrow set of 12 indicators that should be annually reported to Parliament in the context of budgetary discussions.	Agenda-setting, policy formulation, policy evaluation

(continues)

Country	Mechanism	Leading agency	Short description	Stop of the policy cycle targeted
Netherlands	"Accountability Day"	Netherlands Cabinet	The annual "Monitor of Well-Being" produced by the National Statistical Institute will form the basis of Cabinet considerations on the state of well-being in the country. These Cabinet considerations will then be part of the accountability debate in the House of Representatives (in May each year). In addition, the policy assessment agencies in the country (the Netherlands Bureau for Economic Policy Analysis, the Netherlands Environmental Assessment Agency, and the Netherlands Institute for Social Research) are asked to "conduct a periodic exploration of well-being," based on the Monitor.	Agenda-setting
New Zealand	Living Standards Framework	Treasury	The Treasury Living Standards Framework was developed in 2011 as part of an internal process intended to enhance policy advice, and as a response to external criticisms regarding the Treasury's vision. This well-being framework is intended to provide evidence-based advice to Ministers on the lives of New Zealanders, and to be used as input into the policy process, rather than a decision-making tool in itself.	Policy formulation
Scotland	Scotland Performs	Government	The Scottish government's National Performance Framework (NPF), first released as part of the 2007 Spending Review, defines a 10-year vision for the country based upon an outcomes-based approach (rather than inputs and outputs) to measuring the government's achievements. The NPF forms the basis of performance agreements with public service delivery bodies, including at the local level, and is used to monitor their effectiveness.	Monitoring, evaluation

(continues)

Country	Mechanism	Leading agency	Short description	Stop of the policy cycle targeted
Sweden	New Measures for Prosperity	Ministry of Finance	The New Measures of Well-Being developed by the Swedish government as a complement to GDP have been integrated into the Budget Bill 2017.	Agenda-setting, policy evaluation
United Kingdom	The What Works Centre for Wellbeing, various central government activities	The What Works Centre for Wellbeing (an independent agency), various central government departments, previously co-ordinated by the Cabinet Office	Efforts to bring well-being metrics into policy in the United Kingdom have taken several different forms. One is the What Works Centre for Wellbeing, an independent collaborative center that aims to develop and boost the generation of high-quality evidence on well-being for decision makers in government, communities, businesses, and other organizations to use in their work.	Agenda-setting, policy formulation, policy evaluation
United Arab Emirates	The Happiness Policy Manual	Ministry of State for Happiness and Wellbeing, The National Programme for Happiness and Positivity	In October 2017, a Happiness Policy Manual was published but the National Programme for Happiness and Positivity, proposing the use of happiness in policy-making. The approach to implementation is presented through three stages of the policy cycle: policy formulation, policy assessment, and policy implementation.	Whole policy cycle

Source: Exton, C. and M. Shinwell (2018). "Policy use of well-being metrics: Describing countries' experiences," *OECD Statistics and Data Working Paper,* forthcoming, OECD Publishing, Paris.

(in New Zealand). Ecuador and Scotland lie between these two extremes, with a defined number of indicators and well-defined monitoring procedures (through the National Development Plan in Ecuador, and a National Performance Framework in Scotland).

The type of high-level outcome indicators also varies across countries depending on their specific use in the policy process. For example, in Italy one of the criteria for selecting indicators for the budget law was the ability to forecast trends in these indicators in the near future (three years ahead). Because of this criterion, subjective well-being indicators were excluded from the list on account of their limited capacity for data collection, concerns about data quality, and limited evidence on how budgetary decisions could affect their evolution. By contrast, the What Works Centre for Wellbeing in the United Kingdom puts a strong emphasis on subjective well-being measures, and has identified a number of policies that should be changed when such a framework (rather than conventional cost-benefit analysis) is used.

In some countries, well-being policy frameworks have engaged the Parliament, whether or not they were first initiated by the Parliament or government. In France, Italy, and the Netherlands (as well as, to a lesser extent, in Sweden), the goal is that Parliament should have the evidence base needed to hold government accountable for its decisions, through annual reporting of the impacts of their policies on (selected) well-being indicators. In other cases, a central government agency has taken the lead, as in New Zealand, where the Treasury is in charge of the Living Standards Framework, and Ecuador, where the Buen Vivir Secretariat and the Planning Ministry (SENPLADES) acting as lead.

More generally, some of the initiatives presented in Table 4.1 have benefited from strong leadership, often involving a prominent political figure promoting the concept of well-being. A notable example is Ecuador, where former President Rafael Correa initiated a revision of the constitution to incorporate the concept of *buen vivir*. This was also the case in France (with the introduction of a law by a member of the Senate, Eva Sas), in the United Kingdom (with the launch of the Measuring National Wellbeing program by former Prime Minister David Cameron), and in Scotland (following the accession to power of the Scottish National Party in 2007).

Most of these initiatives are quite recent, however, implying that adjustments and modifications are to be expected, and that it is too early to draw lessons. A crucial challenge is whether initiatives taken by one government can survive the election of the next government, especially when the latter comes from a different party or coalition. For this reason, ensuring continuity in political engagement with respect to well-being concepts is essential. This in turn may require using extensive forms of public consultations, so as to build a consensus and coalition in support of the framework that could outlive the incumbent government, or embed the framework in a multi-year development plan. Difficulties can also be compounded when the initiatives are strongly associated with a political figure—i.e., can the actions to implement well-being frameworks outlast their instigator? This most likely depends on whether a "Beyond GDP" approach is strongly supported by the public and mainstreamed within the civil service.

The development of evidence-based policies focused on well-being will also require a continued iterative progress in data collection, dissemination, analysis, and policy experimentation. Sustaining the use of "Beyond GDP" metrics over time is, therefore, a challenge. What steps are necessary in order to mainstream the use of metrics in policy and assure their longevity? What tools are most effective in widening the interest across stakeholders? Here we highlight one challenge—that of attributing changes in one or more well-being variables to a given set of policies.

Demonstrating causality in a public policy context is always difficult. Prime experimental conditions for establishing cause and effect are extremely rare when trying to improve people's lives in a fair and balanced way through policy decisions. Collection of the right kinds of data, at the right time, and use of the most appropriate models and tools can help in building the necessary evidence base. Policies targeted at specific outcomes may inadvertently affect several other outcomes, or generate unintended effects. In the case of well-being metrics, additional challenges for policy are the multidimensional nature of well-being and, as discussed in the previous chapter, the difficulty in identifying inter-linkages between different well-being metrics. For many well-being indicators that have only recently been introduced in large-scale and high-quality data collections in countries' national statistics, it will take time to build the time series needed to investigate policy questions of interest, to enable analytical work and forecasting. Routine inclusion of well-being metrics in studies to evaluate policy impacts is needed to build up the evidence base required.

An additional challenge in the use of a broad well-being framework in developing countries is the concern that this agenda may divert attention away from what is often viewed as fundamental, namely economic growth. A government failing to produce economic growth and an increase in GDP may be tempted to defend its failure by arguing that it was pursuing a broader agenda. This critique needs to be addressed head-on. GDP growth may be necessary to provide the resources needed for strengthening well-being, but it is not sufficient; growth that does not benefit most of the population and that is not sustainable is not "good growth," and it is only within our broader framework that one can ascertain whether growth is, in fact, of the kind that is leading to enhanced societal well-being. As we noted above, short-term growth that is achieved in ways that lead to more inequality, greater environmental degradation, and lower trust is not sustainable.

Use of Subjective Well-Being Data in Policy Analysis

Most of the well-being frameworks described in Table 4.1 include a measure of people's subjective well-being as one among other types of indicators covered. In other words, how people evaluate and experience their life is considered an important element for describing their own well-being, but it is not the sole variable encompassing the influence of all others.

Subjective well-being, however, has features that lend it to specific use in policy analysis. In particular, it has proved responsive to a wide range of objective circumstances, such as income, health, social relations, and political voice. Because of this feature, analysis of the drivers of people's subjective well-being (when based on large samples of respondents and covering many aspects of people's circumstances) can improve policy design and evaluation by highlighting those impacts that are not captured (or only partially so) by standard income or other more objective measures.

Subjective well-being measures are also relevant to determine the nonmonetary costs and benefits of projects and policies, making subjective well-being an important part of the design and evaluation of policy impacts.

Some public programs have collected subjective well-being data among participants to highlight the impact of the policy intervention on program participants. Such evaluations have often highlighted impacts that would have otherwise been missed (Ludwig et al., 2013). Subjective well-being data are also being used in cost-benefit analysis undertaken by public agencies to value nonmonetary costs and benefits (Fujiwara and Campbell, 2011). The approach of the UK Treasury provides an example.

Subjective well-being can also be relevant for policies directed at more specific outcomes, like health. In their chapter in the accompanying volume, Krueger and Stone provide evidence, for instance, that subjective well-being is an important "mediator" for improving outcomes in other fields: it *predicts* people's morbidity and mortality. Policies that enhance people's subjective well-being indirectly achieve a multiplicity of other outcomes. It even affects childbearing and fertility decisions, and the self-esteem of cancer patients. As knowledge on the determinants of subjective well-being progresses, this research will provide policy-makers with additional tools for affecting both subjective well-being and those outcomes that are mediated by it. Even without a full understanding of the determinants of trust and of the multiple and complex relationships that determine outcomes in our complex social/economic/environmental system, there are things that can be done to enhance the likelihood of better societal outcomes.

Conclusions

From the very beginning in our research program, we argued that better and different data and information inevitably shape the political debate. The politics today is different from what it was when we began our work more than a decade ago. It demands information about aspects of our society that were at the time little studied and understood. Our statistical systems need to reflect the concerns of our society—and, to the extent possible, anticipate future concerns. At the time we began our work, there was too little focus either on sustainability or on inequality. Some politicians may have hoped that if we just didn't measure inequality, no one would know the extent to which it was growing. That was naïve and foolish. But now that we know that so little of the fruits of growth over the past decades have gone to the bottom 90%, we can't ignore it. It is part of the political reality that has to be dealt with.

The very progress that has been achieved on measuring well-being following the release in 2009 of the Commission report has contributed to a change in the question that we face, from "How do you develop credible metrics of people's lives?" to "How do you use these metrics in the policy process once you have developed them?" This is a new and more difficult question, but also one that many governments are starting to confront in their day-to-day operations. It is our hope that these applications be pursued and extended to other countries in the future, to allow us to identify the practices that work best in this field.

5.

Twelve Recommendations
on the Way Ahead
in Measuring Well-Being

This chapter argues that the success of the 2009 Stiglitz-Sen-Fitoussi Commission report reflected its capacity to give expression to concerns that were widely shared on the inadequacies of the metrics that are currently used to guide policies, and to provide a vocabulary for linking streams of research that had, until then, been perceived as disconnected. While much remains to be done to translate the recommendations made by the Stiglitz-Sen-Fitoussi report in statistical practice, this short chapter provides a set of 12 new recommendations building on the work done by the HLEG over the past 5 years.

We want to conclude this short book with three general considerations.

First, as we noted already, the range of initiatives that have been put in place since the release of the Commission report in 2009 has gone far beyond the expectations of all of us. We have moved from a "niche," where the assumptions and value judgments hidden in our measurement system were noted in footnotes and quickly forgotten, to a "movement" that is today engaging researchers, policy analysts, Statistical Offices, international organizations, and Treasuries (the traditional gatekeeper of financial orthodoxy). We believe that, beyond any specific argument or recommendation that was included in the Commission's report, this success reflected the capacity of our report to "catch a mood" that was latent in society, giving expression to concerns that were widely shared. The 2009 Commission report also provided a *vocabulary* through which various people could approach this agenda, connecting streams of research that had up to then been perceived as disconnected and sometimes in conflict with each other. It also reconnected academic research and statistical practice, a relation that needs to be maintained in the future.

Second, while the "Beyond GDP" agenda is sometimes characterized as "anti-growth," this is not the philosophy underlying this book. As argued above, the use of a more comprehensive but parsimonious dashboard of indicators reflecting what we value as a society, would have led, most likely, to stronger GDP growth than that actually achieved by most countries in the aftermath of the global financial crisis. What we are arguing is that growth that increases a GDP number but does not reflect an increase in the well-being of most citizens, does not reflect the degradation of the environment and the depletion of natural resources, makes the economy and its citizens more insecure, erodes trust in our institutions and society, and opens up conflicts because of disparate treatment of those of different ethnic or racial groups is not "real" growth. We should not be mesmerized by a number that cannot reflect all of these dimensions. The real growth that should be our focus is growth that is equitable and sustainable.

This means, too, that we are arguing against the narrow view of the economic system as separate from the social and natural environment where it operates, a system where factors of production are always fully used, and where the only policy concern is that of maximizing economic efficiency, i.e., "doing more with less." Standard economic theory almost took it as an axiom that we should be maximizing GDP, conflating that number with societal well-being, ignoring the massive market failures that advances in economic theory over the past century have taught us about. It ignored our planetary boundaries, and the many dimensions of well-being that are not well captured by GDP, that might actually go down as GDP goes up. The "Beyond GDP" agenda has had such global resonance because citizens, and now, at last, economists have widely understood that GDP in itself is not a good measure of well-being, and that our economy is a means to an end, an end of enhancing well-being for all of our citizens today and tomorrow. Perhaps the 2008 financial crisis and the 2016 political crisis have taught a lesson about what happens with too narrow a vision: even GDP may be harmed, but without question, so too will economic performance and social progress rightly understood. Our statistical indicators—the dashboard that we have advocated, based on a national dialogue reflecting the values and circumstances of the country—can play an important role in helping ensure a broader vision. Table A.2 in the Annex, which features indicators from the OECD's *How's Life?* report (OECD, 2017a), provides an example of the types of indicators that could be included in this dashboard.

Third, despite the progress achieved, we are still far from being able to conclude with a declaration of "mission accomplished." Researchers, practitioners, statisticians, opinion shapers, and policymakers will have to keep up the argument and advance this agenda in concrete and practical ways. Despite progress, most of the recommendations included in the 2009 report of the Stiglitz-Sen-Fitoussi Commission remain relevant today, and we hope that further progress in their implementation can be achieved in the future. In the light of the work pursued by the HLEG, we present below a set of 12 recommendations that, we believe, could provide additional directions for future work.

RECOMMENDATIONS BY THE
CHAIRS OF THE HLEG

1. No single metric will ever provide a good measure of the health of a country, even when the focus is limited to the functioning of the economic system. Policies need to be guided by a dashboard of indicators informing about people's material conditions and the quality of their lives, inequalities thereof, and sustainability. This dashboard should include indicators that allow us to assess people's conditions over the economic cycle. Arguably, policy responses to the Great Recession might have been different had such a dashboard been used.

2. Developing better metrics of people's well-being is important for all countries, whatever their level of development. National Statistical Offices should be given the resources and independence needed to pursue this task in effective ways, including through harnessing the potential of big data. The international community should invest more in upgrading the statistical capacities of poorer countries.

3. The quality and comparability of existing metrics of economic inequality related to income and, particularly, wealth should be further improved, including by allowing Statistical Offices to use tax records to capture developments at the top end of the distribution, and by developing measures of the joint distribution of household income, consumption, and wealth.

4. Data should be disaggregated by age, gender, disability status, sexual orientation, education, and other markers

of social status in order to describe group differences in well-being outcomes; and metrics to describe within-household inequalities, such as those related to asset ownership and the sharing of resources and financial decisions within the household, should be developed.

5. Efforts to integrate information on economic inequalities within the System of National Accounts should be pursued, in the perspective of achieving convergence between micro- and macro-approaches, and of understanding how the benefits of GDP growth are shared in society.

6. Assessing equality of opportunity is important. Measures of a broad range of people's circumstances should be developed, including by linking administrative records across generations and by including retrospective questions on parental conditions in household surveys, so as to allow comparison of measures of inequality of opportunity across countries and over time.

7. Regular, frequent, and standardized collection of both evaluative and experiential measures of subjective well-being should be pursued, based on large representative samples with a view to shedding light on their drivers and on the directions of causality.

8. Policies should be routinely assessed for their effects on people's economic insecurity, measured through a dashboard of indicators that inform about people's experiences in the face of economic shocks, the buffers that are available to them, the adequacy of social insurance against key risks, and subjective evaluations of insecurity.

9. Better measures of sustainability are needed. This requires developing full balance sheets for various

institutional sectors, covering all their assets and liabilities, measuring the rents implicit in asset valuations, as well as improved metrics of human and environmental capital and of the vulnerability and resilience of systems.

10. The measurement of trust and other social norms should be improved, through both general and specialized household surveys as well as more experimental tools administered to representative samples of respondents that rely on insights from psychology and behavioral economics.

11. Access to statistical data and administrative records by academics and policy analysts should be facilitated, in ways that preserve the confidentiality of the information disseminated and that ensure a level playing field across different research teams and theoretical perspectives.

12. To deliver "better policies for better lives," well-being metrics should be used to inform decisions at all stages of the policy process, from identifying priorities for action and aligning program objectives to investigating the benefits and costs of different policy options; from making budgeting and financing decisions to monitoring policies, program implementation, and evaluation.

ANNEX: TAKING STOCK OF PROGRESS IN THE "BEYOND GDP" MEASUREMENT AGENDA SINCE THE 2009 COMMISSION REPORT

Since its release in 2009, the Stiglitz-Sen-Fitoussi Commission report has had much resonance within the statistical community, spurring a large number of measurement initiatives worldwide. It has also acted as a catalyst for research, and for communicating the "Beyond GDP" agenda to the general public. We describe some of the key initiatives below, distinguishing between those undertaken by individual countries at the national level and those carried out by international agencies with a more global perspective.

National Initiatives

Many countries have breathed life into the well-being measurement agenda advocated by the Stiglitz-Sen-Fitoussi Commission in 2009 by launching initiatives with frameworks and dashboards of indicators that are now published and updated regularly. While a few of these initiatives predate the release of the Commission report, the report surely accelerated the trend. Table A.1 details the key features of 15 prominent national measurement initiatives explicitly related to the recommendations of the Commission, listing, for each initiative, the type of framework used and the leading agency responsible for compiling the indicators. Although the motivations underlying the development of well-being measurement frameworks differed across countries, some features are notably similar:

- First, all of the frameworks have used a multidimensional approach, typically combining data about people's economic circumstances and material living conditions with indicators that consider a wide range of quality of life factors.
- Second, consulting with wide audiences was often part of these national initiatives. While these consultations were done with varying levels of intensity, focusing on either the indicators or the dimensions included in the framework, they contributed toward building the "legitimacy" of the indicator sets, and to ensuring the longevity of the reporting (see "Public Consultations Within National Measurement Initiatives").
- Third, most of these indicator sets have included measures of people's subjective well-being as one of their key components. Life satisfaction featured most commonly in these national indicators sets, but other types of subjective measures were also sometimes included, such as measures of experiential well-being and eudaemonia. However, in all cases these subjective measures were used as a complement to, rather than as a replacement for, objective indicators.

PUBLIC CONSULTATIONS WITHIN NATIONAL MEASUREMENT INITIATIVES

Several countries have undertaken public consultations as part of the process of developing measurement frameworks relating to well-being. These consultations were held at different stages of the process of establishing the well-being framework, and their inputs have shaped the framework in different ways. While public consultations require time and resources, and can significantly extend the time needed to complete the process of selecting indicators, they also contribute meaningful insight into what matters the most to people in different countries and regions. Examples of consultations undertaken in the context of the well-being initiatives include:

- In Italy, as part of the process launched in 2010 by the Italian Statistical Office (ISTAT) of establishing the BES ("equitable and sustainable well-being") framework, a steering group was established on the "Measurement of Progress in Italian Society," made up of 33 representatives of the business sector, professional associations, trade unions, environmental groups, cultural heritage groups, women's groups, consumer protection groups, and civil society networks. The steering group developed a multidimensional approach to measuring well-being. In addition, a Scientific Commission with 80 researchers and experts from ISTAT, universities, and other institutions was established to consult on this process. Further, a survey representative of the Italian population was conducted (with about

45,000 people interviewed), in which respondents were asked which dimensions are most important for well-being. This was supported by a dedicated website, a blog, and an online survey to consult the public on the committee's decisions (with approximately 2,500 respondents). After the release of the first report, the initiative was presented in a series of meetings in different regions. Since then, ISTAT publishes an annual publication on BES indicators, including composite measures for different thematic domains.

- In New Zealand, the Treasury conducted targeted workshops when developing its Living Standards Framework. In the first round of consultation, held in 2009, workshops (with some 200 participants) were held with government, business, academia, and community groups to get feedback on the proposed framework, on the best ways to communicate about it, and on what themes were most important. An advisory group, including representatives from government and civil society, was created to consult on the framework.[1]

- In Germany, a national dialogue (spread over a period of 6 months) was launched in 2015 to identify the issues that are most important for quality of life in the country and the measures that could be used to describe them.[2] The dialogue, which included several types of public consultation (meetings, online surveys, postcards), involved about 200 meetings held throughout the country with over 8,000 participants. The Chancellor, members of government, and Cabinet

Ministers participated in 50 of these meetings. Civil society, representative organizations, business associations, and trade unions also supported the dialogue. Over 7,000 people responded through the online survey and postcards. Results from this dialogue, together with international comparison and research projects, informed the framework (with 12 dimensions and 46 indicators) that was finally adopted by the government. The framework will be updated on a regular basis.

- In the United Kingdom, the Measuring National Well-being program, launched in November 2010, started with a 6-month National Debate on "what matters," in order to understand what should count as measures of national well-being. The National Debate was carried out by the Office of National Statistics (ONS) and included 175 events held across the country, involving around 7,000 people and more than 34,000 responses, as well as responses from organizations representing many more people. Meetings were also held with citizens, hard-to-reach groups, organizations, charities, experts, the National Statistician's Advisory Forum, and a Technical Advisory Group (ONS, 2011). Following the National Debate, the ONS carried out public consultation on several other well-being measurement issues, including proposals of domains and headline measures, as well as on measures of human and natural capital.

- In Israel, the process for selecting indicators to monitor "Well-Being, Sustainability, and Resilience" included a public consultation process held in parallel with the work of expert groups on each of 9 domains covered by the framework. Following the consultation, two additional domains were added to the framework. The consultation included an online survey (which garnered responses from around 1,600 respondents) and workshops with people lacking access to the internet (which included some 400 participants). Analyses of the responses from these two elements led to a mapping highlighting the dimensions that are most important for quality of life according to respondents. Expert groups comprising representatives of government, the private sector, civil society, labor unions, academia, and other organizations were also set up for each domain.

- In France, following the enactment of a law on "New Wealth Indicators" in 2015, the process of selecting indicators involved a twofold process of consultation. The first part was the establishment of a working group of around 60 people (researchers, representatives of civil society, international organizations, and experts), which established an initial list of themes and indicators. The second part of the process was a wider public consultation, intended to assess the adequacy of the indicators and to prioritize the themes and indicators in order to narrow down the final set. Three types of consultations were held: an online survey, where over 4,000 respondents were asked to order the themes according to their importance; a telephone survey with a representative sample of the total population, where respondents were asked to rank the themes and indicators; and 4 focus groups set up with 10 participants in each, where the approach, themes, and indicators selected were debated.

Conversely, one notable difference among these national initiatives concerned their leadership and motivation. In some countries, responsibility was with the National Statistical Office or similar agencies (e.g., Austria, the Netherlands), suggesting that the underlying rationale of these initiatives was mainly that of providing additional metrics beyond GDP, without necessarily embedding these measures into policy. In other cases, however, measurement frameworks were developed by a center-of-government agency (e.g., the Prime Minister's office in Israel and Sweden; the Federal Chancellery in Germany) or by a combination of policy-related agencies (e.g., Slovenia, Italy, France, Finland), with a clear ambition to use these metrics in policy settings (see Chapter 4).

1. www.stats.govt.nz/browse_for_stats/environment/environmental-economic-accounts/public-sustainable-development-workshop-summary.aspx.

2. https://buergerdialog.gut-leben-in-deutschland.de/DE/Home/home_node.html.

International Initiatives

Work undertaken at the international level has mainly focused on mobilizing existing statistical information and on providing the basis for improving well-being statistics in the future. For example, in 2011, the OECD presented a framework on measuring well-being, largely based on the Commission domains and dimensions (see "The OECD Better Life Initiative"), populated with a number of comparable indicators, for monitoring and benchmarking the performances of its member countries (i.e., to identify strengths and weaknesses). The indicators used were mainly sourced from official statistics but also relied on comparable measures drawn from nonofficial sources (used as "placeholders") for those areas where high-quality official statistics were not yet available. The OECD also released in 2016 a dashboard of indicators of household economic well-being to describe short-term developments in household conditions that could be contrasted to those in quarterly GDP; this comparison highlighted the significant differences over the business cycle between household-level and economy-wide measures.[1]

Similarly, in Europe, the statistical office of the European Union (Eurostat) engaged in a process (in the context of a broader "INSEE-Eurostat" Sponsorship Group on measuring progress, well-being, and sustainable development, launched to respond to the Commission recommendations)[2] that led to the development of a set of Quality of Life Indicators (17 headlines indicators pertaining to 9 dimensions) that are regularly used to monitor conditions in EU member countries (Eurostat, 2017).

The UN Sustainable Development Goals process that led to the adoption of the 2030 Agenda (with its associated goals, targets, and indicators for global monitoring) by the UN General Assembly in 2015 also referred to the importance of building on ongoing efforts to develop measures of progress complementing GDP.[3]

THE OECD BETTER LIFE INITIATIVE

In 2011, the OECD presented its framework for measuring well-being, developed in consultation with the Statistical Offices of its member countries. The framework (Figure A.1) was largely based upon the recommendations of the Stiglitz-Sen-Fitoussi Commission as well as on a variety of other national and international initiatives. It conceptualizes well-being as a multidimensional construct, distinguishing between current well-being and its sustainability over time and, within the former, between material conditions and quality of life. Most of the 11 dimensions of current well-being are those discussed by the Commission report, ranging from health status to education and skills, quality of the local environment, personal security, and subjective well-being, although excluding the dimension of "economic insecurity" (due to lack of suitable indicators) and detailing "material conditions" in terms of three more specific dimensions (income and wealth, jobs and earnings, and housing). As in the Stiglitz-Sen-Fitoussi report, the OECD framework describes sustainability in terms of resources that are critical for future well-being (natural, human, economic, and social capital).

The biennial OECD report *How's Life?* presents a set of internationally comparable well-being indicators for OECD and partner countries pertaining to current well-being, resources for future well-being, and well-being inequalities (describing "vertical inequalities," i.e., the gaps between people at the top and people at the bottom of the distribution; "horizontal inequalities," i.e., gaps between groups of people by gender, age, and education level; and well-being deprivations, i.e., the share of the population falling below a threshold value or standard of well-being). Table A.2 presents the indicators included in the *How's Life?* dashboard. Since its release in 2011, special chapters of *How's Life?* have also provided evidence and analysis on specific themes (gender differences in well-being and job quality in 2013; child well-being, volunteering, and well-being in subnational regions in 2015; migrants' well-being and governance in 2017), as well as identifying priorities for future statistical work in these areas.

Figure A.1. The OECD Well-Being Framework

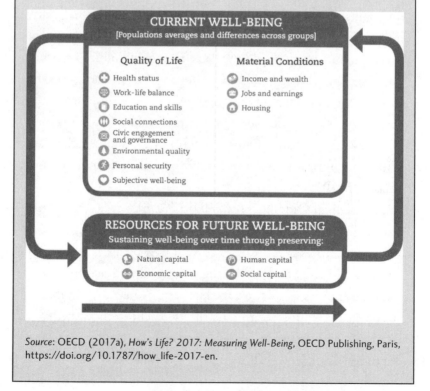

Source: OECD (2017a), *How's Life? 2017: Measuring Well-Being*, OECD Publishing, Paris, https://doi.org/10.1787/how_life-2017-en.

Beyond these initiatives to develop dashboards of indicators, however, a significant part of the work by international organizations has been devoted to creating the basis for improved well-being statistics in the future, with a focus on those areas that currently lack a foundation with official statistics.

- On the environment side, a milestone (described in Chapter 3) was the adoption by the UN Statistical Commission in 2012 of the core accounts of the System of Environmental-Economic Accounting (SEEA) as an international statistical standard, with a companion set of ecosystem accounts recognized as "experimental" (also see Chapter 9 by De Smedt, Giovannini, and Radermacher in the accompanying volume). While the SEEA process predates the Commission report, it tapped into one of its key areas of focus, and countries' efforts to implement the SEEA were boosted by the favorable reaction of the statistical community to the Commission report.

- On the economic side, in 2009 G-20 Finance Ministers and Central Bank Governors endorsed recommendations to address some of the data gaps revealed by the global financial crisis. The initiative, which is led by the Financial Stability Board and the International Monetary Fund, with participation of other international agencies (such as the OECD), is focusing on the monitoring of risk in the financial sector, on the analysis of vulnerabilities, interconnections, and spillovers (including cross-border), and on reflecting information on economic inequalities in macro-economic statistics. Several of these aspects featured prominently in the 2009 report.

- On labor statistics, the 2013 revision of the international standards governing the compilation of labor force surveys explicitly referred to the Commission's recommendations to justify the need to revise and broaden the existing standards in order to better measure people's engagement in different forms of work (paid and unpaid) as well as labor underutilization (ILO, 2013).
- More generally, several international organizations undertook methodological work in areas identified by the Commission.
- The OECD developed a series of statistical guidelines to produce comparable measures in the areas of subjective well-being, wealth inequalities, quality of the working environment, and trust, as well as a framework to allow the joint analysis and measurement of household income, consumption, and wealth.
- Within the UN system, a range of measurement initiatives undertaken by various UN agencies explicitly referred to the Commission report as part of the motivation for work aimed at improving the quality and comparability of existing statistics in specific fields, such as time use (UNECE, 2013) and victimization (UNODC, 2015), at extending their reach to new areas (e.g., governance statistics, with the creation of the Praia Group, a UN city group on governance statistics), and at providing a more comprehensive framework for measuring sustainable development (recommendations by the Conference of European Statisticians, UNECE, 2014).

Communicating Information on Well-Being

While dashboards of headline indicators (the tool advocated by the Commission in 2009) are useful to identify the strengths and weaknesses of individual countries, or changes in countries' conditions over time, they are less than ideal when it comes to communicating with the public (and policy-makers) on a broad range of themes, through indicators that have different scales and interpretation. This has spurred a range of initiatives to develop tools that could provide a more parsimonious description of a country's conditions. The OECD created a standard visual to monitor countries' relative performances that is used in many publications (see example of the Netherlands in Figure A.2), as well as an interactive web platform, the Better Life Index,[4] as a communication tool to engage people in the "Beyond GDP" debate. The Better Life Index addressed one specific recommendation put forward by the Commission.[5] Its website enables users to explore a selection of the OECD's well-being indicators, and to build their own international index of well-being, by rating the dimensions of well-being that matter the most to them. The UNDP, on its side, upgraded its Human Development Index (which relies on indicators for income, health, and education) to capture the effect of inequalities in these dimensions. Several national initiatives have also featured user-friendly, web-based interactive dashboards and data exploration tools, including the German Chancellery's *Government Report on Wellbeing in Germany* and Statistics Austria's *How's Austria?*

Figure A.2. The OECD's *How's Life?* Assessment of the Comparative Strengths and Weaknesses in Average Levels of Current Well-Being, the Netherlands

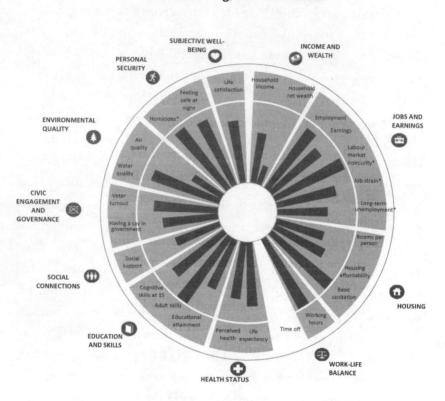

Note: This chart shows the Netherlands' relative strengths and weaknesses in well-being when compared with other OECD countries. For both positive and negative indicators (such as homicides, marked with an "*"), longer bars always indicate better outcomes (i.e., higher well-being), whereas shorter bars always indicate worse outcomes (i.e., lower well-being). If data are missing for any given indicator, the relevant segment of the circle is shaded in white.

Source: OECD (2017a), *How's Life? 2017: Measuring Well-Being*, OECD Publishing, Paris, https://doi.org/10.1787/how_life-2017-en.

Table A.1. Selected National Well-Being Measurement Initiatives and Indicator Sets

Country	Measurement initiative/ indicator set	Leading agency	Short description
Austria	How's Austria	Statistics Austria	Statistics Austria publishes since 2010 an annual report on 30 key indicators categorized into three dimensions: material wealth, quality of life and environmental sustainability. An interactive tool allows users to explore historical trends and compare across indicators.[1]
Belgium	Complementary indicators to GDP	National Accounts Institute	A law adopted In 2014 stipulates that an annual report be published by the National Accounts Institute on Complementary Indicators to GDP, aimed at measuring people's well-being and societal development at the federal level. The report was published in 2016 and 2017, reporting trends for 67 indicators grouped in 13 themes and covering three dimensions: current generation (here and now), future generation (later) and other countries (somewhere else).
Ecuador	Buen Vivir	INEC (Ecuador Statistics Office)	In support of wider work on Buen Vivir, the Ecuador Statistics Office (INEC) compiled a set of indicators to monitor progress.
Finland	Findicator	Statistics Finland and the Prime Minister's Office	Findicator, launched in 2009 by Finland's Prime Minister's Office and Statistics Finland, is an online compendium of over 100 indicators on social progress. A specific category on well-being indicators includes 23 indicators across 8 dimensions.[2]
Germany	Gut Leben in Deutschland	Federal government	The German federal government launched the "Wellbeing in Germany—what matters to us" initiative in response to a commitment of the December 2013 coalition agreement that "We wish to align our policies more closely with the values and hopes of German citizens and we will therefore conduct a dialogue with them in order to gain an understanding of their views on wellbeing issues." Building on a national consultation and based on the findings of other national and international research projects, the initiative includes 46 indicators grouped in 12 dimensions to measure the current status and trends in wellbeing in Germany. The indicators will be updated on a regular basis.[3]

(continues)

Country	Measurement initiative/ indicator set	Leading agency	Short description
Italy	Measures of equitable and sustainable wellbeing	National Council for the Economy and Labour (CNEL) and National Institute of Statistics (ISTAT)	The "Equitable and Sustainable Well-Being" (BES) initiative led to the creation of a well-being framework based on the recommendation of a committee convened by the Italian Prime Minister, which is monitored through a set of indicators and an annual report by ISTAT. A law approved in 2016 stipulated that a narrower framework be developed for reporting to parliament in the context of budgetary discussions.
Israel	Well-being, Sustainability, and National Resilience Indicators	Central Bureau of Statistics	A government resolution approved in April 2015 asked the Central Bureau of Statistics to publish a set of well-being, sustainability, and national resilience indicators. The 2015 resolution included indicators in 10 domains (quality of employment; personal security; health; housing and infrastructure; education; higher education and skills; personal and social well-being; environment; civic engagement and governance; and material standard of living) and called for the development of indicators in 2 additional domains (information technology; and leisure, culture, and community). For each domain, 8 indicators were selected.[4]
Japan	Commission on Measuring Well-Being	Commissioned by government	A Commission on Measuring Well-Being was established in 2010, under the government's Cabinet Office and with participation of experts, to promote research and studies on new growth and well-being, and to develop and improve statistics in these fields as a part of the government's "New Growth Strategy." In December 2011, the Commission released the report Measuring National Well-being—Proposed Well-Being Indicators, whose framework (based on the three domains of socioeconomic conditions, health, and relatedness) was populated through subjective and objective indicators.[5]

(continues)

Country	Measurement initiative/ indicator set	Leading agency	Short description
Luxembourg	Well-Being GDP/ Luxembourg Index of Well-Being	Statec (the National Statistics and Economic Studies Institute), the Economic and Social Council, and the Higher Council for Sustainable Development	The Luxembourg Index of Well-Being ("PIBien-être") was developed through a collaboration between the National Statistics and Economic Studies Institute (Statec), the Economic and Social Council, and the Higher Council for Sustainable Development. It reports on 63 indicators, grouped under 11 domains of life, which closely correspond to the domains of the OECD framework for measuring well-being. In an additional step, these indicators are also summarized through a synthetic index. This is intended to provide a "compass" to guide users through the data, and is used in the 2017 report to evaluate trends in overall well-being, as well as trends in specific domains, since 2009.
Netherlands	Monitor of Well-Being	Central Bureau of Statistics	In 2017, the Cabinet commissioned Statistics Netherlands (CBS) to compile an annual "Monitor of Well-Being" to facilitate public and political debate. Policy assessment agencies—the Netherlands Bureau for Economic Policy Analysis (CPB), the Netherlands Environmental Assessment Agency (PBL), and the Netherlands Institute for Social Research (SCP)—will contribute to the Monitor, and conduct a periodic exploration of well-being based on it. The monitor is based on the "Sustainability Monitor," published by CBS since 2011, which reports on progress on three themes (quality of life here and now; resources for the future; and impacts on other countries) and a total of 9 dimensions.[6]
Scotland	Scotland Performs/National Performance Framework	Scottish Government	The Scottish government's National Performance Framework (NPF) was first released as part of the 2007 Spending Review, providing a 10-year vision for Scotland that uses an outcomes-based approach to measure government's achievements, rather than inputs and outputs. It features 5 strategic objectives, 16 national outcomes, and 55 national indicators. The NPF forms the basis of performance agreements with public service delivery bodies, and is used for monitoring their effectiveness.

(continues)

Country	Measurement initiative/ indicator set	Leading agency	Short description
Slovenia	Indicators of Well-Being in Slovenia	Institute of Macroeconomic Analysis and Development (IMAD), Statistics Slovenia (SURS), Slovenian Environment Agency (ARSO), National Institute of Public Health (NIJZ)	Indicators of Well-Being were developed as part of the National Development Strategy launched by the Slovenian government in 2015 to establish a common vision of Slovenia's future to 2050. The indicator set is implemented by a consortium of four institutions (the Institute of Macroeconomic Analysis and Development, IMAD; the Statistical Office of the Republic of Slovenia, SURS; the Slovenian Environment Agency, ARSO; and the National Institute of Public Health, NIJZ), with indicators grouped under three categories (Material, Social, and Environmental well-being). The indicators are updated once a year, with data presented from 1996.[7]
United Kingdom	Measuring National Wellbeing (MNW) program	UK Office for National Statistics	The MNW, launched in 2010, aims to monitor and report on "how the UK as a whole is doing" through measures of well-being. A progress report is published biannually covering areas including health, natural environment, personal finances, and crime. The measures include objective and subjective data.

1. www.statistik.at/web_en/statistics/------/hows_austria/index.html.
2. www.findikaattori.i/en/hyvinvointi.
3. www.gut-leben-in-deutschland.de/static/LB/en.
4. www.cbs.gov.il/statistical/stat151_eng.pdf.
5. www.cao.go.jp/keitai2/koufukudo/pdf/koufukudosian_english.pdf and www.japanfs.org/en/news/archives/news_id032635.html.
6. http://download.cbs.nl/pdf/2015-a324-pub.pdf and www.cbs.nl/en-gb/news/2017/07/cbs-to-compile-a-monitor-of-well-being.
7. www.kazalniki-blagnje.gov.si/en/wb-slo.html.

Table A.2. Well-Being Indicators Included in *How's Life? 2017*

Panel A. Current well-being, averages

Quality of life	Material conditions

Work-life balance

Working hours (share of employees usually working 50 hours or more per week)

Time devoted to leisure and personal care (hours per day, people in full-time employment)

Income and wealth

Household net adjusted disposable income per capita (USD at current PPP rates)

Household net wealth per household (USD at current PPP rates)

Health status

Life expectancy at birth (number of years that a newborn can expect to live)

Perceived health status (share of adults reporting "good" or "very good" health)

Jobs and earnings

Employment rate (population ages 15–64)

Average annual gross earnings per full-time employee (USD at PPP rates)

Labor market insecurity due to unemployment (average expected earnings loss due to unemployment as a share of previous earnings)

Incidence of job strain (share of employees experiencing a number of job demands exceeding the number of job resources)

Long-term unemployment rate (share of the labor force unemployed for one year or more)

Education and skills

Educational attainment (share of people 26–64 having attained at least upper secondary education)

Competencies of the adult population ages 16–65 (mean proficiency in literacy and numeracy)

Cognitive skills of 15-year-old students (mean score for reading, mathematics, and science)

Housing

Average number of rooms per person (excluding bathroom, toilet, kitchenette, utility rooms, garages)

Housing affordability (share of household gross adjusted disposable income spent on housing rent and maintenance)

Social connections

Social support (share of people who report that they have friends or relatives whom they can count on in times of trouble)

(continues)

Panel A. Current well-being, averages, *continued*

Quality of life	Material conditions

Civic engagement and governance

Voter turnout (percentage of votes cast among the population registered to vote)

Having a say in what the government does (share of people ages 16–65 who feel they have a say in what the government does)

Environmental quality

Water quality (percentage of satisfied people in the overall population)

Air quality (exposure to outdoor air pollution by fine particulate matter, population-weighted mean PM2.5 concentrations, micrograms per cubic meter, 3-year moving average)

Personal security

Homicides (age-standardized prevalence of deaths due to assault)

Feelings of safety (share of people feeling safe when walking alone at night in the city or area where they live)

Subjective well-being

Life satisfaction (mean values on an 0- to 10-point scale)

Panel B. Current well-being, inequalities

Vertical inequalities	Horizontal inequalities (by age, gender, and educational level)	Deprivations
Income and wealth	**Income and wealth**	**Income and wealth**
S80/S20 household disposable income ratio	Gaps in average household disposable income	Relative income poverty
Share of household net wealth of the top 10%	Gaps in average household net wealth	Asset-based poverty
Jobs and earnings	**Jobs and earnings**	**Jobs and earnings**
P90/P10 gross earnings ratio	Gaps in average hourly earnings	Risk of low pay
	Gaps in employment rate	Unemployment rate
	Gaps in unemployment rate	
	Gaps in risk of low pay	
Housing conditions	**Housing conditions**	**Housing conditions**
		Share of people spending more than 40% of disposable income on housing
		Share of households living in overcrowded dwellings
Health status	**Health status**	**Health status**
Standard deviation of age at death	Gaps in self-reported health status	Share of people rating their health status as fair, bad, or very bad
	Difference in life expectancy (years) at age 25 by education level, for men and women	
Work-life balance	**Work-life balance**	**Work-life balance**
S80/S20 hours worked ratio	Gaps in average time devoted to personal care and leisure	Share of employees usually working 50 hours or more per week
S80/S20 ratio in time devoted to personal care and leisure	Gaps in incidence of long working hours	

(continues)

Panel B. Current well-being, inequalities, *continued*

Vertical inequalities	Horizontal inequalities (by age, gender, and educational level)	Deprivations
Education and skills	**Education and skills**	**Education and skills**
P90/P10 PISA scores ratio P90/P10 PIAAC scores ratio	Gaps in share of adults ages 25–64 with upper secondary or tertiary education Gaps in average PISA scores across all fields Gaps in average PISA scores across all fields by the parents' education level Gaps in average PIAAC scores across both fields	Share of adults ages 25–64 with below upper secondary education Share of 15-year-old students who score at or below Level 2 in science, reading, and mathematics (PISA) Share of adults who score at or below Level 1 in both literacy and numeracy (PIAAC)
Social connections	**Social connections**	**Social connections**
S80/S20 ratio in time spent on social activities (among participants)	Gaps in average time spent on social activities Gaps in quality of network support	Share of people who report not having relatives or friends to count on
Civic engagement and governance	**Civic engagement and governance**	**Civic engagement and governance**
S80/S20 political efficacy ratio	Gaps in political efficacy Gaps in self-reported voter turnout	Share of people who consider having no influence on the national government Share of people who have not cast a vote in national elections

(continues)

Panel B. Current well-being, inequalities, *continued*

Vertical inequalities	Horizontal inequalities (by age, gender, and educational level)	Deprivations
Environmental quality	**Environmental quality**	**Environmental quality**
	Gaps in satisfaction with the quality of the water in the local area	Share of people exposed to more than 15 micrograms/m³ of PM2.5 Share of people reporting not to be satisfied with the quality of the water in their local area
Personal security	**Personal security**	**Personal security**
	Gaps in deaths by assault per 100,000 population Gaps in feelings of security when walking alone at night	Deaths by assault per 100,000 population Share of people reporting to not feel safe when walking alone at night
Subjective well-being	**Subjective well-being**	**Subjective well-being**
S80/S20 life satisfaction ratio	Gaps in average life satisfaction	Share of people reporting low life satisfaction Share of people reporting negative affect balance

Panel C. Resources for future well-being

Stocks	Flows	Risks
Natural capital	**Natural capital**	**Natural capital**
Population exposure to outdoor air pollution by fine particulate matter (population-weighted mean PM2.5 concentrations, micrograms per cubic meter, 3-year moving average)*	Greenhouse gas emissions from domestic production (CO_2 equivalent, tons per capita)	
Forest area in square kilometers, per thousand people	Carbon dioxide emissions embodied in domestic final demand (tons per capita)	
Renewable freshwater resources (1,000m3 per capita, long-term annual average)		
Freshwater abstractions (gross abstraction from groundwater or surface water bodies, cubic meters, per capita)		
Threatened species (share of all known species, separately for birds, mammal, and vascular plants)		
Human capital	**Human capital**	**Human capital**
Cognitive skills of 15-year-old students (mean score for reading, mathematics, and science)*	Share of people 25–24 who have attained at least upper secondary education*	Prevalence of smoking (share of people ages 15 and over who report smoking every day)
Adult skills (mean proficiency in literacy and numeracy of the population, ages 16–65)*	Educational expectancy (average number of years in education that a child age 5 can expect to undertake before age 39)	Prevalence of obesity (share of the population ages 15 and older)
Life expectancy at birth (number of years that a newborn can expect to live)*	Long-term unemployment (share of the labor force unemployed for 1 year or more)*	

Panel C. Resources for future well-being, *continued*

Stocks	Flows	Risks
Social capital	**Social capital**	**Social capital**
Trust in others (mean score, on a scale from 0 to 10)	Volunteering (share of the working-age population who declared having volunteered through an organization at least once a month, over the preceding year)	
Trust in the police (mean score, on a scale from 0 to 10)		
Trust in the national government (mean score, on a scale from 0 to 10)		
Voter turnout (percentage of votes cast among the population registered to vote)*		
Government stakeholder engagement when developing primary laws and subordinate regulations		
Economic capital	**Economic capital**	**Economic capital**
Produced fixed assets (USD per capita, at 2010 PPPs)	Gross fixed capital formation (annual growth rates)	Household debt (percentage of net household disposable income)
Financial net worth of the total economy (USD per capita, at current PPPs)	Investment in R&D (percentage of GDP)	Leverage of the banking sector (ratio of selected assets to banks' own equity)*
Intellectual property assets (USD per capita, at 2010 PPPs)		
Household net wealth (USD at current PPPs, per household)*		
Financial net worth of general government (percentage of GDP)		

* Denotes indicators that are also considered headline measures of current well-being.

Source: OECD (2017a), *How's Life? 2017: Measuring Well-Being*, OECD Publishing, Paris, https://doi.org/10.1787/how_life-2017-en.

NOTES

Introduction

1. He also is professor of economics at LUISS Guido Carli University in Rome. From 1989 to 2010 he served as president of the Observatoire Français des Conjonctures Économiques. He is the recipient of a large number of awards, including the Association Française de Science Économique Prix (French Association for Economic Sciences Award) and the Rossi Award from the Académie des Sciences Morales et Politiques (Academy of Moral and Political Sciences). France has recognized his contributions by awarding him the Officier de l'Ordre National du Mérite and Officier de la Légion d'Honneur.

2. Published originally as Stiglitz, J., J. Fitoussi and M. Durand (2018), *Beyond GDP: Measuring What Counts for Economic and Social Performance*, OECD Publishing, Paris, https://doi.org/10.1787/9789264307292-en.

3. I should also acknowledge those who have published the Commission's report in other languages, in particular Xinhua in simplified Chinese, Etas in Italian, Dongnyok in Korean, and RBA in Spanish.

1. The Continued Importance of the "Beyond GDP" Agenda

1. Speech at University of Kansas, March 18, 1968.

2. The picture of the state of the economy provided by these early GDP estimates came as a shock to observers who had, until then, relied on partial data on production, employment, and sales for different industries and regions: for the United States "the volume of net income paid out to individuals shrank by 40% during this (1929–32) three year period" (US Congress, 1934).

3. The joke of Paul Samuelson is famous: "What happens to GDP when a professor marries his servant?"

4. In the same article, Simon Kuznets—moving from the observation that "no one would welcome an acceleration of the overall rate of economic growth that was associated primarily with a market increase in defence expenditure"— argued that "effort must be exerted to formulate a consensus (on a list of desirable

contents of economic growth, omitting the vulgar, the frivolous and the dangerous) . . . and to reformulate it in response to changing conditions" (Kuznets, 1962).

5. Speech at the University La Sorbonne in Paris, September 14, 2009, for the launch of the Commission's report.

6. On October 15, 2007, commenting on "The Recent Financial Turmoil and Its Economic and Financial Consequences" at the Economic Club in New York, Ben Bernanke (Chair of the US Federal Reserve from 2006 to 2014) noted: "The financial system entered the episode of the past few months with strong capital positions and a robust infrastructure. The banking system is healthy. Despite a few notable failures, hedge funds overall seem to have held up well, and their counterparties have not sustained material losses. The clearing and settlement infrastructure generally worked well despite trading volumes that were extremely high in some cases. Nevertheless, the market strains were serious . . . and they posed risks to the broader economy" (www.federalreserve.gov/newsevents/speech /bernanke20071015a.htm). In August 2008, Olivier Blanchard—who was to take up his role as IMF chief economist on the following month—wrote about the state of macro-economics as a field, concluding that "the state of macro is good" (Blanchard, 2009). This was just as the economics profession as a whole failed to anticipate the most significant macro-economic event in three-quarters of a century, with the dominant DSGE (dynamic stochastic general equilibrium) model saying that a crisis of such features and proportion couldn't or wouldn't happen. They were unable to provide the analytic framework to address the crisis, including answering key policy questions. It was a financial crisis, and yet in the standard DSGE model the banking system, the wider financial system, credit rationing, or liquidity made no significant appearance. Perhaps even more remarkable, *after* the depth and severity of the crisis became apparent, Bernanke would write that there had been nothing wrong with the underlying models, only with their implementation (Lectures at Princeton University, Bernanke, 2014).

7. Comments made by Alan Greenspan at the Economic Club of New York on May 20, 2005. Greenspan also noted: "Without calling the overall national issue a bubble, it's pretty clear that it's an unsustainable underlying pattern," with "a lot of local bubbles" around the country (www.federalreserve.gov/boarddocs /speeches/2005/200505202/default.htm).

8. The need to develop data on institutional balance sheets was recognized by the G20 as part of the G20 Data Gaps Initiative, led by the IMF and the Financial Stability Board, and implemented by several international organizations. The G20 Data Gaps Initiative includes 23 recommendations. Recommendation II.8

(on sectoral accounts, including "from-whom-to-whom" information, i.e., financial relations by sector of origin and destination) and recommendation II.9 (about incorporating information on distribution in the System of National Accounts household account) are led by the OECD.

9. US quarterly GDP growth for the 3rd and 4th quarter of 2009, which was originally estimated by the Bureau of Economic Analysis at -0.5% (actual rate) was revised downward 3 years later (in steps) to -1.6%. The final estimate for average GDP growth over these two quarters was finally set at -1.3%.

10. In the euro area, GDP per capita increased by a cumulative 0.7% from 2009 to 2012, while household disposable income per capita fell over the same period by 0.7%, i.e., a gap of 1.8 points. The gap was larger in countries most affected by the Great Recession (e.g., in Spain real GDP contracted over the same period by 1.6% while household income fell by 3.6%) while it had the opposite sign in a few OECD countries—e.g., in the US, growth of real household income (at 1.5%) slightly exceed that of real GDP (at 1.3%).

11. The transfer of intellectual property assets within multinational enterprises was significantly incentivized by Ireland's favorable tax system.

12. There were many other factors contributing to the growing lack of trust, and there are, to our knowledge, no good studies parsing out the relative role of these factors. For instance, many commentators cite the lack of accountability of the bankers, who were viewed as causing the crisis—the bailouts centered on the banks rather than helping those who had suffered from predatory lending. Thus, there was a sense that the decisions about the response to the crisis were often in the hands of the very people who had brought on the crisis. This increased the sense that people have little control over what their government does: on average, only one-third of people in OECD countries feel that they have some influence on what their government does (OECD, 2017b, p. 183). For a more extensive discussion of trust, see Chapter 10 by Yann Algan in the companion volume and Chapter 3 in this volume.

13. The Commission had as one of its central missions ensuring that our metrics drew our attention to those things that made a difference in the lives of ordinary people.

14. The members of the Commission were Bina Agarwal, University of Delhi; Kenneth J. Arrow, Stanford University; Anthony B. Atkinson, Nuffield College, Oxford; François Bourguignon, Paris School of Economics; Jean-Philippe Cotis, INSEE; Angus S. Deaton, Princeton University; Kemal Dervis, UNPD; Marc Fleurbaey, Université Paris 5; Nancy Folbre, University of Massachusetts; Jean

Gadrey, Université de Lille; Enrico Giovannini, OECD; Roger Guesnerie, Collège de France, Paris; James J. Heckman, Chicago University; Geoffrey Heal, Columbia University; Claude Henry, Sciences-Po/Columbia University; Daniel Kahneman, Princeton University; Alan B. Krueger, Princeton University; Andrew J. Oswald, University of Warwick; Robert D. Putnam, Harvard University; Nick Stern, London School of Economics; Cass Sunstein, University of Chicago; and Philippe Weil, Sciences-Po, Paris.

15. Assuming that there exist complete markets for future goods as well.

16. Abramovitz (1959) noted: "Since Pigou . . . economists have generally distinguished between . . . welfare at large, and the narrower concept of economic welfare," with "national product taken to be the objective and measurable counterpart of economic welfare." Easterlin (1974) further noted that Arthur Pigou first expressed the "clear presumption that changes in economic welfare indicate changes in social welfare in the same direction, if not in the same degree."

17. www.oecd-6wf.go.kr/eng/main.do.

18. www.oecd.org/statistics/better-life-initiative.htm.

19. In his final State of the Union Address in 2016, President Obama described rising income inequality as the "defining challenge of our time" (www.nytimes.com/2016/01/13/us/politics/obama-2016-sotu-transcript.html).

20. www.oecd.org/sdd/measuring-distance-to-the-sdgs-targets.htm.

21. See Doyle and Stiglitz (2014). Condensed and reprinted in the *Ministers Reference Book: Commonwealth 2015* (London: Henley Media Group), pp. 86–88.

22. See, for example, the Slovenian National Development Strategy: www.vlada.si/en/projects/slovenian_development_strategy_2030/.

23. Within Europe, several Statistical Offices have taken steps to account for "quality changes" in the volume measures for various types of government services (Eurostat, 2016).

24. This work is being pursued through a collaboration between the OECD and IMF.

25. Also published in French by Odile Jacob under the title *Richesse des nations et bien-être des individus*, in Chinese (reduced version) by Xinhua, in Italian by Etas, in Korean by Dongnyok, and in Spanish by RBA.

26. Following the French initiative, the G20 Leaders released a statement in Pittsburgh (November 2009) and Toronto (June 2010) encouraging "work on measurement methods so as to better take into account the social and environmental dimensions of economic development." In Europe, the EU Commission

issued a communication to the European Council and Parliament in 2009 on "GDP and beyond: Measuring progress in a changing world," which referred to the Commission report. This communication identified five concrete actions aimed at (1) complementing GDP with better environmental and social indicators; (2) developing (near) real-time information for decision making; (3) reporting more accurate information on distribution and inequalities; (4) developing a European scoreboard on sustainable development; and (5) extending the National Accounts to cover environmental and social issues.

2. The Measurement of Economic Downturns

1. The previous chapter noted that GDP metrics typically rely on market prices to assess the relative value of different goods and services, and normally it is impossible for national accounts statisticians to determine whether there is some distortion in pricing. Still, there should perhaps be a warning about the use of GDP to assess how well the economy is doing when there is the possibility of a bubble, especially in real estate: "Use with extreme caution."

2. Of course, many did: for instance, the IMF warned of unsustainable current account imbalances, and many others warned about unsustainable public debt. Ironically, it was not these imbalances that brought down the economy, but something more mundane, and historically more familiar: bad and excessive lending by the financial sector, and an accumulation of private debt.

3. In the United States, for example, the median sale prices for new homes increased by 130% from 1995 to 2016, while median (equivalized) household disposable income increased by 80% (in nominal terms). Over the same period, the median size of new single-family houses increased from 178 to 225 square meters. As noted by Robert H. Frank, in the United States good schools (whose budgets are typically funded by local property taxes) are located in more expensive neighborhoods, implying that "any family that failed to rent or purchase a house near the median of its local price distribution would have to send its children to below-average schools" (Frank, 2011).

4. Since 2015, the OECD has been releasing measures of over-indebtedness of households based on different thresholds (i.e., debt-to-income above 3, and debt-to-assets above 0.75). For a recent analysis, see Balestra and Tonkin (2018).

5. There are numerous policy actions that the government, including the Federal Reserve, could have taken had it had an adequate appreciation of the economy's financial fragility. Indeed, some of the actions it took may actually have increased the economy's fragility.

6. Beyond the reasons we emphasize here, preliminary estimates of GDP systematically underestimate the *revised* estimates, for technical reasons, for instance related to the entry of new firms and exit of old firms. These need further study, and appropriate corrections introduced. Real-time estimates of GDP based on scraping data from the internet may provide a check against such systematic errors in the future (Buono et al., 2017, pp. 118–120).

7. Sustainability of well-being requires an increase in wealth *appropriately measured*. If wealth is increasing, then later generations can sustain the same level of well-being that is prevailing now, but not so if wealth is decreasing. Wealth includes economic capital (which includes both physical and immaterial items, such as knowledge and research), human capital, natural capital (natural resources and the environment), and social capital (i.e., how well members of a society cooperate with each other).

8. Gaps of similar size are visible when comparing current levels of GDP per capita with those implied by the precrisis growth of "potential output"—the level of GDP that could be expected to prevail based on the long-term drivers of economic growth. Since 2007, OECD estimates of the (annual) growth of potential output were revised downward from 2.7% (mid-2007) to 1.7% (mid-2018) for the United States, and from 1.9% to 1.4% for the euro area.

9. One aspect of physical capital normally not measured, which may increase more than normal during recessions, is associated with maintenance: with greater free time, workers may spend more time on repair and maintenance.

10. OECD (2001) defines human capital as "the knowledge, skills, competencies and attributes embodied in individuals that facilitate the creation of personal, social and economic well-being."

11. When firms are cash starved, they may also cut back on formal on-the-job training. Unfortunately, again, there are no good statistics assessing the level or changes in these expenditures, though in some countries and in some firms they are likely to be quite significant.

12. There is a long-standing controversy about the benefits and costs of an economic downturn, with some, like Joseph Schumpeter, arguing that recessions and depressions have a cleansing effect, forcing firms to become more efficient. Stiglitz (1994) argues that the adverse effects on learning and R&D outweigh these "agency" benefits.

13. But note the observation made earlier in the context of education: in the countries most affected by the crisis, GDP per capita decreased, and so even if the share of health education in GDP held up, spending per capita went down. Austerity typically forced significant cuts in public health expenditures.

14. Sitaraman (2017) describes how some financial institutions have grown so powerfully economically that they can now evade law enforcement, even when taking part in illegal activities, by paying fines.

15. In the United States, they may have borrowed heavily—on average, a college graduate has some $37,000 in student debt (www.forbes.com/sites/zackfriedman /2018/06/13/student-loan-debt-statistics-2018/#1efa9ee87310). The amount of student debt is much higher for some degrees: according to a 2017 Gallup survey, 60% of those who completed their law degree in 2010 or later report borrowing more than $100,000, compared with around half of those who graduated in the 2000s and a quarter of law graduates in the 1990s (http://www.accesslex .org/sites/default/files/2018-01/Examining%20Value%2C%20Measuring%20 Engagement%20-%20A%20National%20Study%20of%20the%20Long -Term%20Outcomes%20of%20a%20Law%20Degree.pdf).

16. OECD (2013d) reports, based on data from the *Gallup World Poll*, that average life satisfaction declined by more than 20% in Greece and by between 12% and 10% in Italy and Spain, as compared with gains by more than 4% in Germany, Israel, Mexico, the Russian Federation, and Sweden. The same report refers to "evidence of growing feelings of anger, stress and worry and lower feelings of joy and contentment in many OECD countries" (p. 88).

17. Assume that the gap between actual and potential GDP is 10% of GDP, and that this gap persists in the future; discounting these future losses at a conservative long-run real interest rate of 2% implies that the present value of the loss in GDP is five times GDP—in the case of Europe and the United States, some $300 trillion.

18. A number of recent articles highlight the permanent effect of recessions on the level of output but not on output growth. For example, Cerra and Saxena (2008), after their analysis of 190 countries over the period 1960–2001, conclude that, following all crises, GDP reverts to its previous growth path.

19. Fernald et al. (2017) for the United States, and Antolin-Diaz, Drechsel, and Petrella (2017) for G7 countries.

20. In addition, multipliers in deep downturns are, almost by definition, much greater than when the economy is near full employment, when an increase in government spending has to be offset by a contraction somewhere else. In deep downturns, central banks don't need to raise interest rates (in the 2008 crisis, they didn't) as government spends more; hence, there is no crowding out of private spending. Indeed, there may be crowding in, as expectations of higher GDP lead to more investment and consumption. The empirical analysis by Caggiano et al. (2015) confirms that fiscal multipliers in a deep recession are much higher than

those observed in an expansionary period—that the deeper the recession, the greater the amount of output generated by a fiscal expansion; and that government spending is very effective when it is most needed (in their estimates, one extra dollar spent by the US government during the Great Recession would have generated higher output of up to $2.50 in three years' time).

21. Originally, the 3% deficit limit and 60% debt limits were set as conditions of entry into the euro area. They subsequently were adopted as criteria for acceptable macro-economic policies.

22. This conclusion may not be shared by all. Public investments may require long planning horizons, so undertaking them in a rush in a recession may result in lower-quality projects (implying that good policy design entails having an inventory of projects to be undertaken should the economy go into a downturn). More generally, the mistrust of governments and their propensity to spend leads some to the view that the only productive investment is the one entrusted to the private sector. Empirical research, however, shows that, on average, investments in both technology and infrastructure, for instance, have high return, markedly in excess of the government's cost of capital.

23. The US global balance sheet position moved from a negative balance of 7% of GDP in 2007 to 32% in 2017 (OECD Annual National Accounts database, https://stats.oecd.org/Index.aspx?DataSetCode=NAAG). Interestingly, some of the money that was invested in the United States from abroad was invested in low-yield assets, and some of the money that the United States invested abroad was invested in high-yield assets, so that the country's net asset position deteriorated by less (25 percentage points of GDP, over the 10 years to 2017) than one would have expected given its recurrent current account deficits (whose cumulative value was equivalent to 27 percentage points of GDP), which require it to get funds abroad year after year.

24. See https://ec.europa.eu/ireland/news/key-eu-policy-areas/economy_en. Looking beyond gross public debt, Barnes and Smyth (2013) show that the net financial liabilities of the Irish general government increased by 81 points of GDP from 2007 to 2012; also, by 2012 the nonfinancial assets of the Irish general government were equivalent to 35% of GDP, while its banking-related contingent liabilities amounted to 73% of GDP.

25. Most educational expenditures, though, create private assets, not public assets; the government's "claim" is only that associated with its ability to capture tax revenues. Still, as we explain above, the government's overall balance sheet may improve under a broad range of circumstances.

26. There is also a concern that those categories of expenditure not included within the capital budget will be given short shrift.

27. Such a behavior was strongly encouraged by the government in some countries, e.g., the Netherlands in the 1980s, the aim being to lower the unemployment rate by moving unemployed workers from unemployment benefits to disability or early retirement schemes.

28. Total hours worked declined in Italy by 6% from 2009 to 2014, and then recovered by around 3%. In the United States, total hours worked declined marginally in 2010, and then increased continuously in later years, with a cumulative rise of 10% over 2009–16 (OECD Employment Outlook database, www.oecd .org/employment/emp/onlineoecdemploymentdatabase.htm).

3. The Need to Follow Up on the Stiglitz-Sen-Fitoussi Commission

1. $1.90 is the updated value of the earlier $1 a day standard for extreme poverty.

2. The OECD generally reports its measures of income poverty based on a threshold set at half of median (equivalized) disposable income, i.e., around $82 per day for a single mother of two children in the United States (i.e., $27 per day per capita). This does not imply that "extreme poverty" (based on the conventional World Bank threshold) has been eradicated in developed countries. Deaton (2018) argues, based on World Bank data, that of the 769 million people who lived on less than $1.9 a day in 2013, 3.2 million were in the United States, and 3.3 million in other OECD countries. Edin and Shaeffer (2016), based on data from the US Census Bureau Survey of Income and Program Participation, report that 4.3% of American households with children (and 5.1% of those without children) reported living on less than $ 2 a day per person in 2011 based on their pretax money income; and that 1.6% (and 4.3%) were in the same condition based on a welfare metric that included food stamps and other welfare benefits.

3. According to Milanovic (2016), the value of the global Gini coefficient (based on household survey data for some 120 countries and 2005 purchasing power parity[PPP]) declined from around 0.72 in 1988 to 0.67 in 2008. Historical estimates of the global Gini coefficient compiled by Bourguignon and Morrison (2002) and by Moatsos et al. (2014)—based on measures of GDP per capita for countries' mean income, on 1990s PPPs, and on measures of within-

country inequalities from a variety of sources—show a continuous increase from the 1820s (with Gini values of around 0.50) to the 1950s (0.67) followed by broad stability thereafter.

4. As noted by Milanovic, measuring global income inequality is a recent endeavor, with estimates affected by factors such as the quality of income distribution data available for individual countries, the PPP wave used, and whether national-account based corrections for differences in mean incomes between surveys and national accounts are applied or not.

5. See OECD Income Distribution Database, www.oecd.org/social/income-distribution-database.htm.

6. The Stolper-Samuelson theorem (Stolper and Samuelson, 1949) predicted that opening up trade between developed and less-developed countries would lower wages in the developed countries, especially those of unskilled workers, even taking into account the lower prices that consumers would have to pay.

7. Whether these programs directly improve the well-being of their parents is debatable. The assumptions used in conventional incidence analysis imply that they do, as they consider the costs of these programs as an income stream accruing to the household participating in them.

8. The use of adjusted income as welfare metric raises its own interpretative problems. Poor households in rural areas will not benefit from health and education services that are mainly benefiting richer households in urban neighborhoods, so that "attributing" these services to them through inadequate techniques would simply overstate their economic well-being. The same upward bias would result from analysis that attributes to end users the higher costs of health care services.

9. The problems associated with discrepancies between macro (national accounts) and micro measures of mean household income are discussed in the next section of this chapter.

10. Capital gains are excluded from the standard definition of household income provided by the UN *Canberra Group Handbook on Household Income Statistics*, 2nd edition. That said, in standard economic analysis, capital gains would count as "income" in the same way as a dividend does.

11. This undercoverage of some hard-to-reach population groups provides one possible explanation of the difference between income measured from surveys and from the national accounts (see below).

12. In the System of National Accounts, all household expenditures on durables are recorded as consumption at the time of the purchase.

13. Drawing on findings from experiments carried out in Tanzania (with 8 random samples of 5,000 households each drawn from the same population), Beegle et al. (2012) concluded that, relative to a benchmark household budget survey with a 14-day recall period and a long list of consumption items, reducing the recall period by a week lowered measured mean consumption by 12%, while combining a lower recall period and a shorter list of commodity items reduced mean consumption by 28%.

14. The OECD has started to collect data on wealth distribution based on its *Guidelines for Micro Statistics on Household Wealth* (OECD, 2013e). The first wave of the OECD Wealth Distribution Database included 17 countries; the second wave released in 2018 extended the coverage to 27 countries. See www.oecd.org /statistics/guidelines-for-micro-statistics-on-household-wealth-9789264194878 -en.htm; and https://stats.oecd.org/Index.aspx?DataSetCode=WEALTH.

15. Even the direction of change in wealth inequality may differ according to whether one captures wealth not held directly by the individual. There is not only the problem of lack of disclosure. Sometimes, the trust documents deliberately obscure who is the beneficiary, naming several individuals who *might* benefit. Only the trustees know who is likely to benefit from the trust. Nevertheless, Kopczuk and Saez (2004) have argued that wealth held in trust is small relative to total household wealth and that its omission does not affect their results on wealth inequalities.

16. The OECD and Eurostat, in association with a number of National Statistical Offices, are currently producing experimental estimates of the joint distribution of household income, consumption, and wealth, based on the OECD Framework for Statistics on the Distribution of Household Income, Consumption and Wealth, www.oecd.org/statistics/framework-for-statistics-on-the-distribution of -household-income-consumption-and-wealth-9789264194830-en.htm.

17. While imputed rents are included in the 2011 "operational definition" of household income proposed by the *Canberra Group Handbook* (UNECE, 2011), several Statistical Offices in OECD countries (Canada, Korea, New Zealand, and the United States) do not routinely include them in their income distribution statistics. Even in countries that do include them, methodological differences (e.g., on the residences included, methods of estimation, types of renters) are so large as to prevent meaningful comparisons across countries.

18. This is partly because there are complex issues associated with assessing the general equilibrium incidence of different taxes and subsidies, which is particularly relevant in assessing the distributional impacts of different policies.

19. Assessments conducted by the IMF (and the World Bank) are based on the fiscal incidence tools developed by the Commitment to Equity Institute. The CEQ, founded in 2015 at Tulane University, has so far developed tax and benefits models for 43 countries (with work in progress for another 23) based on methodologies described in the *CEQ Handbook*. See http://commitmentoequity.org/.

20. For instance, previous investments also benefited from the tax cut, implying negative distributional effects with no positive impact on incentives.

21. A large group of Keynes's followers, led by Cambridge economist Nicholas Kaldor, did give primacy to the importance of distribution in the determination of the macro-economic equilibrium. This tradition survives, and in the aftermath of the 2008 crisis, the Commission of Experts on Reforms of the International Monetary and Financial System, appointed by the President of the United Nations General Assembly, emphasized the role of growing inequality in the crisis. Its final report is available as *The Stiglitz Report: Reforming the International Monetary and Financial Systems in the Wake of the Global Crisis,* (New York: The New Press, 2010). Published in complex Chinese by Commonwealth Magazine Company, in simplified Chinese by Xinhua, in French by Odile Jacob, in India by Orient Blackswan (2011), in Korean by Dongnyok, in Russian by International Relations Publishing, and in Spanish by RBA.

22. Stiglitz provides a theoretical investigation of the relationship between inequality and macro-stability (Stiglitz, 2012a and 2012b). Other empirical and theoretical studies have shown that, *other things being equal,* more inequality undermines economic performance, leading to lower growth and more instability. Cingano (2014), for example, shows that more inequality is associated with greater inequality of opportunity, which means that children at the bottom are less likely to get the human capital they need to live up to their potential. Of course, some countries, like China, have grown very fast in spite of high levels of inequality; indeed, the high GDP growth rate, with parts of the country "pulling ahead" of the rest, contributed to higher inequality.

23. Luck also plays an important role in determining people's life beyond either "circumstances" and "effort." Frank (2016) shows how the role of luck becomes more important in winner-takes-all societies, arguing that the tendency for "successful people . . . to understate luck's role in their success" makes them less willing to invest in achieving public goods.

24. Krueger, statement delivered (in his capacity as Chairman of the Council of Economic Advisers to US President Obama) on January 12, 2012, at the Center for American Progress. https://milescorak.files.wordpress.com/2012/01/34af5d01.pdf.

25. Krueger, in his 2012 statement, labeled this the "Great Gatsby" relationship. Chetty and his co-authors have shown that a similar relationship holds when looking across counties in the United States (Chetty et al., 2018).

26. A simple interpretation of this relationship is that when the rungs of the ladder are further apart (as they are in societies with greater inequality of outcomes), it is harder to move up the ladder.

27. Such long time series are especially important if we want to establish whether income dynamics are Markovian, i.e., whether there are effects that stretch across generations. In the case of Sweden, for which there is some data, there is evidence of such effects (Adermon, Lindhal, and Palme, 2016).

28. A major determinant of economic insecurity is economic volatility; but the effects on insecurity of a given variability in, say, GDP may differ, depending not just on the buffers available but also on the structure of the economy. Germany, for example, responded to the 2008 financial crisis with more work-sharing, so that the risks were more effectively shared among workers than in other countries.

29. In practice, however, the indicators that may be used to monitor some aspects of sustainability (e.g., measures of people's health status or education to measure human capital) may be the same as those used to monitor current well-being.

30. A recent international commission reviewed the evidence and noted that, if the world is to attain the goals it has set for itself of limiting global warming to between 1.5 and 2 degrees Celsius, a tax of at least $50 to $100 per ton of carbon will have to be imposed (CPLC, 2017).

31. One could even say that, along with the theory, they also delivered "its complete mode of use."

32. Within the System of National Accounts, output at current prices of financial intermediaries is measured through an indirect measure of the value of intermediation services with no explicit charge provided by banks (known as "FISIM"). In practice, this is done by applying the difference between the observed interest rates on loans and a risk-free "reference rate" to the amount of outstanding bank loans, and the difference between the observed interest rates on deposit and the risk-free rate to the amount of bank deposits (Lequiller and Blades, 2014).

33. By applying the SEEA framework, monetary and physical data can be combined in a consistent manner for calculating intensity and productivity ratios. Macro-level indicators can also be broken down by industry, which allows one to analyze environmental pressures exerted by different industries and consumption behaviors, and to distinguish government responses from those of the business sector or private households.

34. See, for example, the physical supply table for air emissions that reports emissions (in tons) of 14 substances (ranging from carbon dioxide to ammonia and particulates) from industries (by sector), households (by activity), and land-fills. Similarly, the physical asset account for mineral and energy resources reports opening stocks, additions (discoveries, upward reappraisals, reclassifications), reductions (extractions, catastrophic losses, downward reappraisals, reclassifications) and closing stocks of five types of natural resources (oil, natural gas, coal and peat, and nonmetallic and metallic minerals), with information separately provided for "commercially recoverable resources," "potentially commercially recoverable resources," and "non-commercial and other known deposits" (United Nations et al., 2014).

35. The SEEA Ecosystem Accounts define ecosystems as a "dynamic complex of plant, animal and micro-organism communities and their living environment interacting as functional unit" (United Nations et al., 2014).

36. For an overview of the treatment of mineral and energy resources in the SEEA framework and of the challenges related to the valuation of these resources, see www.oecd-ilibrary.org/docserver/3fcfcd7f-en.pdf?expires=1533647411&id=i d&accname=guest&checksum=5887745A4C5EC338EABCF35528EFE5B1.

37. In the sense of Bourdieu and Passeron (1990).

38. According to data from the Comparative Study of Electoral Preferences (CSES), reported in OECD (2017a), the gap in voter turnout, based on self-reports, between people in the bottom and top income quintile across 25 OECD countries, is around 15 points. These measures are likely to underestimate differentials in voting behavior, as those who did not vote are less likely to report it in surveys.

39. Based on data from the OECD Survey of Adult Skills (OECD, 2013f) reported in OECD (2017a).

40. A similar conclusion was made by the *Voices of the Poor* project, to which we referred earlier in this chapter: lacking voice in decisions that affect their lives was one of the important deprivations reported by the poor (Narayan et al., 2000).

41. A process is currently in place to develop metrics for monitoring progress in attaining Goal 16 of the UN 2030 agenda, which is about "effective and account-able institutions." The Praia Group, a UN city group on governance statistics, has also been created to move forward statistical work in this field.

42. Some policy-makers argued that saving banks, bankers, and their share-holders was necessary to keep the flow of credit going, and that this could be

done even without imposing conditions of "good behavior" (e.g., lending) on the banks. Such policies—protecting bankers rather than ordinary citizens—only undermined further trust in government.

43. Careful attention, however, needs to be given to the mechanisms by which education builds trust. To the extent that it enhances citizens' ability to understand the rationale for government actions—a particular policy can be understood as more than a special measure advancing the interest of some group—it is natural that more education enhances trust. But if government policies largely serve the interests of elites, moving more individuals into the elite through education may increase the number of people who support the government, but will do little to improve trust among the non-elites. Thus, as we have emphasized throughout this book, a "Beyond GDP" analysis requires more granular data than just "averages." More generally, correlation is not causation, and there are often multiple interpretations for why one might expect a particular correlation, with markedly different policy implications.

4. Country-Experiences with Using Well-Being Indicators to Steer Policies

1. As we complete this report, the discussion in several countries on "fake news" presents a challenge to the concept of evidence-based research. Years of statistical research (both methodological and applied) have provided a sound foundation for judging the quality of empirical research, including ascertaining the extent to which something more than correlation has been established. All research, particularly in social sciences, is tentative and potentially refutable by subsequent studies, and good science provides indicators of the confidence by which a given result is held. Thus, we know few things with absolute certainty, while we know some things with a high degree of confidence. One of the contributors to the current lack of trust in the elite is that many made policy pronouncements that were well beyond those that could be made with a reasonable degree of confidence, e.g., that globalization would lead most, if not all, citizens to be better off in a relatively short period of time. This is a case where economic theory had provided a strong argument to the contrary, and where insufficient efforts were made to reconcile empirical studies based on limited data with these broader theoretical perspectives.

2. "Here and now" (current well-being), "later" (capital), and "elsewhere" (transboundary impacts) are the three dimensions drawn from the seminal Brundtland Report (United Nations, 1987) underpinning the conceptual categorization

of sustainable development indicators put forward by the Conference of European Statisticians (UNECE, 2014).

3. https://whatworkswellbeing.org.

Annex

1. The quarterly indicators used by the OECD refer to real household disposable income, net cash transfers from governments to households, real household consumption expenditure, consumer confidence, households' savings rate, households' indebtedness, financial net worth, unemployment, and labor underutilization rates. See www.oecd.org/sdd/na/household-dashboard.htm.

2. The final report of the Sponsorship Group, released in November 2011 following its adoption by the European Statistical System Committee, identified around 50 actions to be taken by the European Statistical System. The report stressed the need for the European Statistical System to use a multidimensional approach when defining quality of life, to develop indicators measuring sustainability, and to use complementary indicators coming from National Accounts that would better reflect the situation of households. Since 2012, these actions have been integrated and gradually implemented in the European Statistical Program.

3. In Article 38 of the final resolution of the United Nations Conference on Sustainable Development, held in Rio de Janeiro in June 2012, member states recognized "the need for broader measures of progress to complement gross domestic product in order to better inform policy decisions. . . . In this regard we request the United Nations Statistical Commission, in consultation with relevant United Nations system entities and other relevant organizations, to launch a program of work in this area, building on existing initiatives."

4. www.oecdbetterlifeindex.org.

5. Recommendation 8 was that "Statistical Offices should provide the information needed to aggregate across quality of life dimensions, allowing the construction of different indexes."

BIBLIOGRAPHY

Abramovitz, M. (1959), "The welfare interpretation of secular trends in national income and product," in Abramovitz, M. (ed.), *The Allocation of Economic Resources—Essays in Honor of Bernard Francis Haley*, Stanford University Press, Stanford, CA.

Adermon, A., M. Lindhal, and M. Palme (2016), "Dynastic human capital, inequality and intergenerational mobility," *IFAU Working Paper*, No. 2016/19, Institute for Evaluation of Labour Market and Education Policy, Uppsala, Sweden, www.ifau.se/en/Press/Abstracts/dynastic-human-capital -inequality-and-intergenerational-mobility/.

Ahmad, N., J. Ribarsky, and M. Reinsdorf (2017), "Can potential mismeasurement of the digital economy explain the post-crisis slowdown in GDP and productivity growth?," *OECD Statistics Working Papers*, No. 2017/09, OECD Publishing, Paris, http://dx.doi.org/10.1787/e751b7-en.

Ahmad, N. and P. Schreyer (2016), "Measuring GDP in a digitalised economy," *OECD Statistics Working Papers*, No. 2016/07, OECD Publishing, Paris, https://doi.org/10.1787/5jlwqd81d09r-en.

Algan, Y. and P. Cahuc (2014), "Trust, growth and well-being: New evidence and policy implications," in Aghion, P. and S. Durlauf (eds.), *Handbook of Economic Growth*, Vol. 2, Elsevier/North-Holland, Amsterdam, pp. 49–120.

Allen, F. and D. Gale (2000), *Comparing Financial Systems*, MIT Press, Boston.

Altimir, O. (1987), "Income distribution statistics in Latin America and their reliability," *Review of Income and Wealth*, Vol. 33(2), pp. 111–155.

Anand, S., P. Segal, and J.E. Stiglitz (eds.) (2010), *Debates on the Measurement of Global Poverty*, Oxford University Press, Oxford.

Antolin-Diaz, J., T. Drechsel, and I. Petrella (2017), *Review of Economics and Statistics*, Vol. 99(2), pp. 343–356, www.mitpressjournals.org/doi/pdf/10.1162 /_a_00646.

Arrow, K.J. (1972), "Gifts and exchanges," *Philosophy & Public Affairs*, Vol. 1(4), pp. 343–362.

Arrow, K.J. and G. Debreu (1954), "Existence of an equilibrium for a competitive economy," *Econometrica*, Vol. 22(3), pp. 265–290, www.jstor.org/stable /1907353.

Atkinson, A.B. (2016), *Monitoring Global Poverty: Report of the Commission on Global Poverty*, The World Bank, Washington, DC.

Atkinson, A.B. (2015), *Inequality—What Can Be Done?*, Harvard University Press, Boston.

Atkinson, A.B. (1970), "On the measurement of inequality," *Journal of Economic Theory*, Vol. 2(3), pp. 244–263.

Atkinson, A.B. and T. Piketty (eds.) (2007), *Top Incomes over the Twentieth Century—A Contrast Between Continental European and English-Speaking Countries*, Oxford University Press, Oxford and New York.

Baily, M.N., J. Manyika, and S. Gupta (2013), "U.S. productivity growth: An optimistic perspective," *International Productivity Monitor*, No. 25, p. 3–12.

Balestra, C. and R. Tonkin (2018), "Inequalities in household wealth across OECD countries: Evidence from the OECD Wealth Distribution Database," *OECD Statistics Working Papers*, No. 2018/01, OECD Publishing, Paris, https://doi.org/10.1787/7e1bf673-en.

Barnes, S. and D. Smyth (2013), "The Government's balance sheets after the crisis: A comprehensive perspective," Irish Fiscal Advisory Council, Dublin.

Bartik, T.J. and B. Hershbein (2018), "Degrees of poverty: The relationship between family income background and the returns to education," *Upjohn Institute Working Paper*, No. 18/284, W.E. Upjohn Institute for Employment Research, Kalamazoo, MI, https://doi.org/10.17848/wp18-284.

Battiston, S. et al. (2013), "Complex derivatives," *Nature Physics*, Vol. 9, pp. 123–125.

Battiston, S. et al. (2012), "Liaisons dangereuses: Increasing connectivity, risk sharing, and systemic risk," *Journal of Economic Dynamics and Control*, Vol. 36(8), pp. 1121–1141.

Beegle, K. et al. (2012), "Methods of household consumption measurement through surveys: Experimental results from Tanzania," *Journal of Development Economics*, Vol. 98 (1), pp. 3–18.

Bernanke, B.S. (2014), *The Federal Reserve and the Financial Crisis*, Princeton University Press, Princeton.

Blanchard, O.J. (2009), "The state of macro," *Annual Review of Economics*, Annual Reviews, Vol. 1(1), pp. 209–228.

Blanchard, O.J. and D. Leigh (2013), "Growth forecast errors and fiscal multipliers," *American Economic Review*, Vol. 103(3), Papers and Proceedings of the One Hundred Twenty-Fifth Annual Meeting of the American Economic Association, pp. 117–120.

Bourdieu, P. and J.C. Passeron (1990), *Reproduction in Education, Society and Culture* (2nd ed.), Sage Publications, Thousand Oaks, CA.

Bourguignon, F. (2012a), *La mondialisation des inégalités*, Seuil, Paris.

Bourguignon, F. (2012b), "Inequality, globalization, and technical change in advanced countries: A brief synopsis," in Catao, L. and M. Obstfeld (eds.), *Globalization's Challenges*, Princeton University Press, Princeton.

Bourguignon, F. and C. Morrisson (2002), "Inequality among world citizens: 1820–1992," *American Economic Review*, Vol. 92(4), pp. 727–744.

Browning, M., P.-A. Chiappori, and Y. Weiss (2014), *Economics of the Family*, Cambridge Surveys of Economic Literature, Cambridge University Press, Cambridge, https://doi.org/10.1017/CBO9781139015882.

Brynjolfsson, E. and A. McAfee (2011), *Race Against the Machine: How the Digital Revolution Is Accelerating Innovation, Driving Productivity, and Irreversibly Transforming Employment and the Economy*, Digital Frontier Press, Lexington, MA.

Buono, D. et al. (2017), "Big data types for macroeconomic nowcasting," *Eurona—Eurostat Review of National Accounts and Macroeconomic Indicators*, pp. 94–144, https://ec.europa.eu/eurostat/cros/system/files/euronaissue1-2017-art4.pdf.

Burkhauser, R.V., J. Larrimore, and K.I. Simon (2012), "A 'second opinion' on the economic health of the American middle class," *National Tax Journal*, Vol. 65(1), pp. 7–32.

Caggiano, G. et al. (2015), "Estimating fiscal multipliers: News from a nonlinear world," *Economic Journal*, Vol. 125(584), pp. 746–776.

Case, A. and A. Deaton (2015), "Rising morbidity and mortality in midlife among white non-Hispanic Americans in the 21st century," *PNAS (Proceedings of the National Academy of Sciences of the United States of America)*, Vol. 112(49), pp. 15078–15083, https://doi.org/10.1073/pnas.1518393112.

CEA (2016), "The long-term decline in prime-age male labor force participation," The Council of Economic Advisers, Washington D.C.

Cerra, V. and S.C. Saxena (2008), "Growth dynamics: The myth of economic recovery," *American Economic Review*, Vol. 98(1), pp. 439–457, www.aeaweb.org/articles?id=10.1257/aer.98.1.439.

Chetty, R. et al. (2018), "Race and economic opportunity in the United States: An intergenerational perspective," *NBER Working Paper*, No. 24441, www .nber.org/papers/w24441.

Cingano, F. (2014), "Trends in income inequality and its impact on economic growth," *OECD Social, Employment and Migration Working Papers*, No. 163, OECD Publishing, Paris, https://doi.org/10.1787/5jxrjncwxv6j-en.

Corak, M. (2013), "Income inequality, equality of opportunity, and intergenerational mobility," *Journal of Economic Perspectives*, Vol. 27(3), pp. 79–102.

Coyle, D. (2013), "The cost of mistrust," in *OECD Yearbook 2013*, OECD Publishing, Paris, https://doi.org/10.1787/observer-v2012-5-en.

CPLC (2017), *Report of the High-Level Commission in Carbon Prices*, Carbon Pricing Leadership Coalition, The World Bank, Washington, DC.

Currie, J. (2009), "Healthy, wealthy, and wise: Socioeconomic status, poor health in childhood, and human capital development," *Journal of the Economic Literature*, Vol. 47(1), pp. 87–122.

Dasgupta, P. and I. Serageldin (eds.) (2000), *Social Capital: A Multifaceted Perspective*, World Bank, Washington, DC.

Deaton, A. (2018), "The U.S. can no longer hide from its deep poverty problem," *New York Times*, www.nytimes.com/2018/01/24/opinion/poverty-united -states.html (accessed on September 18, 2018).

Deaton, A. (2013), *The Great Escape: Health, Wealth and the Origins of Inequality*, Princeton University Press, Princeton.

Deaton, A. (2005), "Measuring poverty in a growing world (or Measuring growth in a poor world)," *Review of Economics and Statistics*, Vol. 87(1), pp. 1–19.

Deaton, A. (1997), *The Analysis of Household Surveys: A Microeconometric Approach to Development Policy*, The World Bank, Washington, DC.

Deepa, N. et al. (2000), *Voices of the Poor: Can Anyone Hear Us?*, Oxford University Press, New York, http://documents.worldbank.org/curated/en/13144 1468779067441/Voices-of-the-poor-can-anyone-hear-us.

De Neve, J.-E. (2018), "Work and well-being: A global perspective," in *Global Happiness Policy Report*, Global Happiness Council, UAE, https://s3 .amazonaws.com/ghc-2018/UAE/GHPR_Ch5.pdf.

Doyle, M. and J.E. Stiglitz (2014), "Eliminating extreme inequality: A sustainable development goal, 2015–2030," *Ethics and International Affairs*, Vol. 28(1), www.ethicsandinternationalaffairs.org/2014/eliminating-extreme -inequality-a-sustainable-development-goal-2015-2030/.

Easterlin, R.A. (1974), "Does economic growth improve the human lot? Some empirical evidence," in David, P.A. and M.W. Reder (eds.), *Nations and Households in Economic Growth: Essays in Honor of Moses Abramovitz*, Academic Press, New York.

Edin, K.J. and H.L. Shaefer (2016), *$2.00 a Day: Living on Almost Nothing in America*, Houghton Mifflin Harcourt, New York.

European Commission (2018), *Pension Adequacy Report 2018* , vol. 1, *Current and Future Income Adequacy in Old Age in the EU*, European Commission, Brussels, http://ec.europa.eu/social/main.jsp?=738&langId=en&pubId =8084&furtherPubs=yes.

EuroMOMO (2018), "European mortality bulletin week 22, 2018," European Monitoring of Excess Mortality for Public Health Action, Copenhagen.

Eurostat (2017), *Final Report of the Expert Group on Quality of Life Indicators*, https://publications.europa.eu/en/publication-detail/-/publication/1c2fee3e -15d5-11e7-808e-01aa75ed71a1/language-en.

Eurostat (2016), *Handbook on Prices and Volume Measures in National Accounts—2016 Edition*, Publication Office of the European Union, Luxembourg, http://ec.europa.eu/eurostat/documents/3859598/7152852/KS-GQ -14-005-EN-N.pdf.

Exton, C. and M. Shinwell (2018), "Policy use of well-being metrics: Describing countries' experiences," *OECD Statistics and Data Working Paper*, forthcoming, OECD Publishing, Paris.

Exton, C., C. Smith, and D. Vandendriessche (2015), "Comparing happiness across the world: Does culture matter?," *OECD Statistics Working Papers*, No. 2015/04, OECD Publishing, Paris, http://dx.doi.org/10.1787/jrqppzd9bs2-en.

Fernald, J.G. et al. (2017), "The disappointing recovery of output after 2009," *NBER Working Paper*, No. 23543, National Bureau of Economic Research, www.nber.org/papers/w23543.

Fisher, J. et al. (2016), "Inequality in 3D: Income, consumption and wealth," *Working Paper Series*, No. 2016-09, Washington Center for Equitable Growth, Washington, DC, http://cdn.equitablegrowth.org/wp-content /uploads/2017/12/21123945/122117-WP-Inequality-in-3D.pdf.

Fitoussi, J.-P and P. Rosanvallon, (1996), *Le nouvel âge des inégalités*, Seuil, Paris.

Fitoussi, J.-P. and F. Saraceno (2014), "Drivers of inequality: Past and present challenges for Europe," Sciences-Po Publications, http://spire.sciencespo.fr /hdl:/2441/2q6hk56t1k8o6qje4l40fj5s9t/resources/2014-fitoussi-saraceno -drivers-of-inequality.pdf.

Fitoussi, J.-P. and J.E. Stiglitz (2013), "On the measurement of social progress and wellbeing: Some further thoughts," *Global Policy*, Vol. 4(3), pp. 290–293.

Fitoussi, J.-P. and X. Timbeau (2011), "Financial sustainability of an economy: exploratory remarks," *OFCE Working Paper*, No. 2011-14, Centre de recherche en économie de Sciences-Po, http://spire.sciencespo.fr/hdl:/2441/5l6uh8ogmqildh09h561k0hj4/resources/wp2011-14.pdf.

Frank, R.H. (2016), *Success and Luck: Good Fortune and the Myth of Meritocracy*, Princeton University Press, Princeton.

Frank, R.H. (2011), "Supplementing per-capita GDP as measure of well-being," paper presented at the American Economic Association meeting in Denver, CO.

Fujiwara, D. and R. Campbell (2011), "Valuation techniques for social cost-benefit analysis: Stated preference, revealed preference and subjective well-being approaches," Department for Work and Pensions, HM Treasury, London.

Garrouste, C. and M. Godard (2016), "The lasting health impact of leaving school in a bad economy: Britons in the 1970s recession," *Health Economics*, Vol. 25(2), pp. 70–92.

Gordon, R. (2016), *The Rise and Fall of American Growth—The U.S. Standard of Living Since the Civil War*, Princeton University Press, Princeton.

Greif, A. (1994), "Cultural beliefs and the organization of society: A historical and theoretical reflection on collectivist and individualist societies," *Journal of Political Economy*, Vol. 102, pp. 912–950.

Greif, A. (1993), "Contract enforceability and economic institutions in early trade: The Maghribi traders' coalition," *American Economic Review*, Vol. 83(3), pp. 525–548.

Hacker, J. (2018), "Economic security," in Stiglitz, J.E., J.-P. Fitoussi, and M. Durand (eds.) (2018), *For Good Measure: Advancing Research on Well-Being Metrics Beyond GDP*, OECD Publishing, Paris.

Haldar, A. and J.E. Stiglitz (2016), "Group lending, joint liability, and social capital: Insights from the Indian microfinance crisis," *Columbia Business School Research Paper*, No. 17-19, https://ssrn.com/abstract=2905302.

Heckman, J. and D.V. Masterov (2004), "The productivity argument for investing in young children," *Working Paper*, No. 5, Committee for Economic Development, Washington, DC.

Helliwell, J.F., R. Layard, and J.D. Sachs (eds.) (2018), *World Happiness Report 2018*, Sustainable Development Solutions Network, New York, http://worldhappiness.report/ed/2018/.

HM Treasury (2018), *The Green Book: Appraisal and Evaluation in Central Government*, www.gov.uk/government/publications/the-green-book-appraisal -and-evaluation-in-central-governent.

ILO (2013), Resolution Concerning Statistics of Work, Employment and Labour Underutilization, adopted by the Nineteenth International Conference of Labour Statisticians, October 2013, www.ilo.org/global/statistics-and -databases/standards-and-guidelines/resolutions-adopted-by-international -conferences-of-labour-statisticians/WCMS_230304/lang--en/index.htm.

IMF (2017), *Fiscal Monitor—Tacking Inequality*, International Monetary Fund, Washington, DC.

IMF (2013), "Ex post evaluation of exceptional access under the 2010 Stand-By Arrangement," *IMF Country Report*, No. 13/156, Washington, DC.

Inchauste, G. and N. Lustig (eds.) (2017), *The Distributional Impact of Taxes and Transfers: Evidence from Eight Low- and Middle-Income Countries*, World Bank, Washington, DC.

Inglehart, R.F. and P. Norris (2016), "Trump, Brexit, and the rise of populism: Economic have-nots and cultural backlash," *HKS Faculty Research Working Paper*, No. 16-026, Harvard Kennedy School, Cambridge, MA.

Kahn, L.B. (2010), "The long-term labor market consequences of graduating from college in a bad economy," *Labour Economics*, Vol. 17, pp. 303–316.

Kahneman, D. and A. Deaton (2010), "High income improves evaluation of life but not emotional well-being," *Proceedings of the National Academy of Sciences*, Vol. 107(38), pp. 16489–16493.

Kahneman, D. and A. Tversky (1984), "Choice, values, and frames," *American Psychologist*, Vol. 39(4), pp. 341–350, http://dx.doi.org/10.1037/-066X.39 .4.341.

Kentikelenis, A. et al. (2014), "Greece's health crisis: From austerity to denial-ism," *The Lancet*, Vol. 383(9918), pp. 748–753.

Kharas, H. and B. Seidel (2018), "What's happening to the world income distribution? The Elephant chart revisited," *Global Economy and Development Working Paper*, No. 114, Brookings, Washington, DC.

Kopczuk, W. and E. Saez (2004), "Top wealth shares in the United States, 1916–2000: Evidence from estate tax returns," *National Bureau of Economic Research Working Paper*, No. 10399.

Krueger, A.B. (2017), "Where have all the workers gone? An inquiry into the decline of the U.S. labor force participation rate," *Brookings Paper Economic Activity Conference Draft*, Washington, DC.

Kuznets, S. (1962), "How to judge quality," *New Republic*, Vol. 147. pp. 29–32.

Layard, R. et al. (2014), "What predicts a successful life? A life-course model of well-being," *Economic Journal*, Vol. 124(580), pp. F720–F738.

Lequiller, F. and D. Blades (2014), *Understanding National Accounts* (2nd ed.), OECD Publishing, Paris, https://doi.org/10.1787/9789264214637-en.

López-Calva, L.F. and N. Lustig (eds.) (2010), *Declining Inequality in Latin America: A Decade of Progress?*, Brookings Institution Press and UNDP, Washington, DC.

Lucas, R. (2004), "The industrial revolution—Past and future, 2003 annual report essay," *Federal Reserve Bank of Minneapolis*, May Issue, pp. 5–20.

Ludwig, J. et al. (2013), "Long-term neighbourhood effects on low-income families: Evidence from Moving to Opportunity," *American Economic Review*, Vol. 103(3), pp. 226–31.

Lustig, N. (2018), "The sustainable development goals, domestic resource mobilization, and the poor," in Ocampo, J.A. and J.E. Stiglitz (eds.), *The Welfare State Revisited*, Columbia University Press, New York.

Meadows, D.H. et al. (1972), *The Limits to Growth—A Report for the Club of Rome's Project on the Predicament of Mankind*, Universe Books, New York.

Milanovic, B. (2016), *Global Inequality: A New Approach for the Age of Globalization*, Harvard University Press, Cambridge, MA.

Moatsos, M. et al. (2014), "Income inequality since 1820," in Van Zanden, J. et al. (eds.), *How Was Life?: Global Well-Being Since 1820*, OECD Publishing, Paris, https://doi.org/10.1787/9789264214262-15-en.

Murtin, F. et al. (2018), "Trust and its determinants: Evidence from the Trustlab experiment," *OECD Statistics Working Papers*, No. 2018/02, OECD Publishing, Paris, https://doi.org/10.1787/869ef2ec-en.

Narayan, D. et al. (2000), *Can Anyone Hear Us?*, The World Bank, Washington, DC.

OECD (2018a), *OECD Economic Outlook*, Volume 2018, Issue 1, OECD Publishing, Paris, https://doi.org/10.1787/eco_outlook-v2018-1-en.

OECD (2018b), *The Role and Design of Net Wealth Taxes in the OECD*, OECD Tax Policy Studies, No. 26, OECD Publishing, Paris, https://doi.org/10.1787/9789264290303-en.

OECD (2018c), *A Broken Social Elevator? How to Promote Social Mobility*, OECD Publishing, Paris, https://doi.org/10.1787/9789264301085-en.

OECD (2018d), *OECD Labour Force Statistics 2017*, OECD Publishing, Paris, https://doi.org/10.1787/oecd_lfs-2017-en.

OECD (2018e), *OECD Compendium of Productivity Indicators 2018*, OECD Publishing, Paris, https://doi.org/10.1787/pdtvy-2018-en.

OECD (2018f), *OECD Productivity Statistics (database)*, http://dx.doi.org/10.1787/data-en.

OECD (2017a), *How's Life? 2017: Measuring Well-Being*, OECD Publishing, Paris, https://doi.org/10.1787/how_life-2017-en.

OECD (2017b), *OECD Guidelines on Measuring Trust*, OECD Publishing, Paris, http://dx.doi.org/10.1787/-en.

OECD (2017c), "Education database: Educational expenditure by source and destination," *OECD Education Statistics (database)*, https://doi.org/10.1787/1c1c86c4-en (accessed on October 16, 2018).

OECD (2017d), "Health expenditure and financing: Health expenditure indicators (Edition 2017)," *OECD Health Statistics (database)*, https://doi.org/10.1787/828a6dbd-en (accessed on October 16, 2018).

OECD (2015a), *In It Together: Why Less Inequality Benefits All*, OECD Publishing, Paris, http://dx.doi.org/10.1787/-en.

OECD (2015b), *How's Life? 2015: Measuring Well-Being*, OECD Publishing, Paris, https://doi.org/10.1787/how_life-2015-en.

OECD (2013a), *New Sources of Growth: Knowledge-Based Capital—Synthesis Report*, OECD Publishing, Paris, www.oecd.org/sti/inno/knowledge-based-capital-synthesis.pdf.

OECD (2013b), *PISA 2012 Results: Excellence Through Equity (Volume II): Giving Every Student the Chance to Succeed*, PISA, OECD Publishing, Paris, https://doi.org/10.1787/9789264201132-en.

OECD (2013c), *OECD Guidelines on Measuring Subjective Well-Being*, OECD Publishing, Paris, http://dx.doi.org/10.1787/-en.

OECD (2013d), "Well-being and the global financial crisis," in *How's Life? 2013: Measuring Well-Being*, OECD Publishing, Paris, https://doi.org/10.1787 /how_life-2013-7-en.

OECD (2013e), *OECD Guidelines for Micro Statistics on Household Wealth*, OECD Publishing, Paris, https://doi.org/10.1787/9789264194878-en.

OECD (2013f), *OECD Skills Outlook 2013: First Results from the Survey of Adult Skills*, OECD Publishing, Paris, https://doi.org/10.1787/9789264204256 -en.

OECD (2008), *Growing Unequal? Income Distribution and Poverty in OECD Countries*, OECD Publishing, Paris, https://doi.org/10.1787/97892640441 97-en.

OECD (2001), *The Well-Being of Nations: The Role of Human and Social Capital*, OECD Publishing, Paris, http://dx.doi.org/10.1787/-en.

ONS (2011), *Measuring What Matters: National Statistician's Reflections on the National Debate on Measuring National Well-Being*, The Office for National Statistics, London.

Oreopoulos, P., T. von Wachter, and A. Heisz (2012), "The short- and long-term career effects of graduating in a recession," *American Economic Journal: Applied Economics*, Vol. 4, pp. 1–29.

Ostry, J., A. Berg, and C.G. Tsangarides (2014), "Redistribution, inequality, and growth," IMF Staff Discussion Note 14/02, www.imf.org/external/pubs/ft /sdn/2014/sdn1402.pdf.

Palma, J. (2016), "Do nations just get the inequality they deserve? The 'Palma Ratio' re-examined," *Cambridge Working Papers in Economics*, No. 1627, University of Cambridge, Cambridge, https://doi.org/10.17863/CAM.1089.

Pew Research Center (2017), "Historical trends of public trust," www.people -press.org/2017/12/14/public-trust-in-government-1958-2017.

Pew Research Center (2015), "Historical trends of public trust," www.people -press.org/2015/11/23/1-trust-in-government-1958-2015.

Piketty, T. (2014), *Capital in the 21st Century*, Harvard University Press, Cambridge, MA.

Putnam, R. (2000), *Bowling Alone: The Collapse and Revival of American Community*, Simon and Schuster, New York.

Putnam, R., R. Leonardi, and R.Y. Nanetti (1993), *Making Democracy Work. Civic Traditions in Modern Italy*, Princeton University Press, Princeton.

Rockström, J. et al. (2009), "Planetary boundaries: Exploring the safe operating space for humanity," *Ecology and Society*, Vol. 14(2), p. 32, www .ecologyandsociety.org/vol14/iss2/art32/.

Roukny, T., S. Battiston, and J.E. Stiglitz (2017), "Interconnectedness as a source of uncertainty in systemic risk," *Journal of Financial Stability*, Vol. 35, pp. 93–106, https://doi.org/10.1016/j.jfs.2016.12.003.

Saez, E. (2016), "Striking it richer: The evolution of top incomes in the United States (updated with 2015 preliminary estimates)," https://eml.berkeley.edu /~saez/saez-UStopincomes-2015.pdf.

Schreyer, P. and M. Reinsdorf (2018), "Measuring consumer inflation in a digital economy," *OECD Statistics and Data Working Papers*, forthcoming, OECD Publishing, Paris.

Sitaraman, G. (2017), *The Crisis of the Middle-Class Constitution: Why Economic Inequality Threatens Our Republic*, Alfred A. Knopf, New York.

Steffen, W. et al. (2015), "Planetary boundaries: Guiding human development on a changing planet," *Science*, Vol. 347(6223), http://science.sciencemag.org /content/347/6223/1259855.full.

Steptoe, A., A. Deaton, and A.A. Stone (2015), "Subjective wellbeing, health, and ageing," *The Lancet*, Vol. 385(9968), pp. 640–648.

Stern, N. (2006), *The Economics of Climate Change—The Stern Review*, Cambridge University Press, Cambridge.

Stevenson, B. and J. Wolfers (2012), "Subjective well-being and income: Is there any evidence of satiation?," *American Economic Review*, Vol. 103, pp. 598–604.

Stiglitz, J.E. (2016a), "America's great malaise and what to do about it," *Journal of Policy Modeling*, Vol. 38, pp. 639–648, paper presented at the American Economic Association Annual Meetings, San Francisco, www.sciencedirect .com/science/article/pii/S0161893816300412.

Stiglitz, J.E. (2016b), "An agenda for sustainable and inclusive growth for emerging markets," *Journal of Policy Modeling*, Vol. 38, pp. 693–710, paper presented at the American Economic Association Annual Meetings, San Francisco, www.sciencedirect.com/science/article/pii/S0161893816300503.

Stiglitz, J.E. (2015), *Rewriting the Rules of the American Economy: An Agenda for Growth and Shared Prosperity*, Roosevelt Institute, New York, https:// community-wealth.org/sites/clone.community-wealth.org/files/downloads /report-stiglitz.pdf.

Stiglitz, J.E. (2014), "The measurement of wealth: Recessions, sustainability and inequality," in Stiglitz, J.E. and M. Guzman (eds.), *Contemporary Issues in Macroeconomics: Lessons from the Crisis and Beyond*, IEA Conference Volume, No. 155-II, Houndmills, UK, and Palgrave Macmillan, New York (paper presented at a special session of the International Economic Association World Congress, Dead Sea, Jordan, June 2014).

Stiglitz, J.E. (2012a), *The Price of Inequality: How Today's Divided Society Endangers Our Future*, W.W. Norton, New York.

Stiglitz, J.E. (2012b), "Macroeconomic fluctuations, inequality, and human development," *Journal of Human Development and Capabilities*, Vol. 13(1), pp. 31–58.

Stiglitz, J.E. (2010), *The Stiglitz Report: Reforming the International Monetary and Financial Systems in the Wake of the Global Crisis*, The New Press, New York.

Stiglitz, J.E. (2009), "Simple formulae for optimal income taxation and the measurement of inequality," in Basu, K. and R. Kanbur (eds.), *Arguments for a Better World: Essays in Honor of Amartya Sen*, vol. 1, *Ethics, Welfare, and Measurement*, Oxford University Press, Oxford, pp. 535–566.

Stiglitz, J.E. (1994), "Endogenous growth and cycles," in Shionoya, Y. and M. Perlman (eds.), *Innovation in Technology, Industries, and Institutions*, University of Michigan Press, pp. 121–156.

Stiglitz, J.E., J.-P. Fitoussi and M. Durand (eds.) (2018), *For Good Measure: Advancing Research on Well-Being Metrics Beyond GDP*, OECD Publishing, Paris.

Stiglitz, J.E. and B.C. Greenwald (2016), *Creating a Learning Society—A New Approach to Growth, Development, and Social Progress*, Columbia University Press, New York.

Stiglitz, J. E. and B.C. Greenwald (2003), *Towards a New Paradigm in Monetary Economics*, Cambridge University Press, Cambridge.

Stiglitz, J.E., A. Sen, and J.-P. Fitoussi (2009), *Mismeasuring Our Lives: Why GDP Doesn't Add Up*, The New Press, New York.

Stiglitz, J.E., A. Sen, and J.-P. Fitoussi (2009), *Report by the Commission on the Measurement of Economic and Social Progress*, http://ec.europa.eu/eurostat/documents/118025/118123/Fitoussi+Commission+report.

Stolper, W.F. and P.A. Samuelson (1949), "Protection and real wages," *Review of Economic Studies*, Vol. 9(1), pp. 58–73, https://doi.org/10.2307/2967638.

Stone, A.A. and C. Mackie (2015), *Subjective Well-Being: Measuring Happiness, Suffering, and Other Dimensions of Experience*, National Academies Press, Washington, DC.

UNECE (2014), "Conference of European Statisticians recommendations on measuring sustainable development," Geneva, www.unece.org/fileadmin /DAM/stats/publications/2013/CES_SD_web.pdf.

UNECE (2013), *Guidelines for Harmonizing Time-Use Surveys*, United Nations, New York and Geneva, www.unece.org/fileadmin/DAM/stats/publications /2013/TimeUseSurvey_Guidelines.pdf.

UNECE (2011), *The Canberra Group Handbook on Household Income Statistics* (2nd ed.), Geneva, UN, www.unece.org/fileadmin/DAM/stats/groups/cgh /Canbera_Handbook_2011_WEB.pdf.

United Nations (2015), Report of the Secretary-General: A promotion of sustained economic growth and sustainable development, www.un.org/sg/en /content/sg/report-secretary-general-promotion-sustained-economic-growth -and-sustainable-0.

United Nations (1987), *Our Common Future—Report of the World Commission on Environment and Development*, United Nations, New York.

United Nations et al. (2014), *System of Environmental-Economic Accounting 2012—Central Framework*, https://unstats.un.org/unsd/envaccounting /seearev/seea_cf_final_en.pdf.

United Nations et al. (2014), *System of Environmental-Economic Accounting 2012—Experimental Ecosystem Accounting*, https://unstats.un.org/unsd /envaccounting/seeaRev/eea_final_en.pdf.

UNODC (2015), "International classification of crime for statistical purposes," United Nations, Vienna, www.unodc.org/documents/data-and-analysis /statistics/crime/ICCS/ICCS_English_2016_web.pdf.

US Congress (1934), "National income, 1929–32," 73rd Congress, 2d session, S. Doc. 124.

Weichselbaumer, D. and R. Winter-Ebmer (2005), "A meta-analysis of the international gender wage gap," *Journal of Economic Surveys*, Vol. 19(3), pp. 479–511.

Woolley, F. (2004), "Why pay child benefits to mothers?," *Canadian Public Policy /Analyse de Politiques*, Vol. 30(1), University of Toronto Press, pp. 47–69.

Zucman, G. (2015), *The Hidden Wealth of Nations. The Scourge of Tax Havens*, University of Chicago Press, London.

HIGH-LEVEL EXPERT GROUP ON THE MEASUREMENT OF ECONOMIC PERFORMANCE AND SOCIAL PROGRESS

Chairs

Joseph E. Stiglitz, Professor of Economics, Business and International Affairs, Columbia University

Jean-Paul Fitoussi, Professor of Economics at Sciences-Po, Paris and LUISS University, Rome

Martine Durand, Chief Statistician, OECD

Members

Yann Algan, Professor of Economics, Sciences-Po, Paris

François Bourguignon, Paris School of Economics

Angus Deaton, Senior Scholar and Dwight D. Eisenhower Professor of Economics and International Affairs Emeritus, Woodrow Wilson School of Public and International Affairs and Economics Department, Princeton University

Enrico Giovannini, Professor of Economic Statistics, University of Rome Tor Vergata

Jacob Hacker, Director of the Institution for Social and Policy Studies, and Stanley B. Resor Professor of Political Science, Yale University

Geoffrey Heal, Garrett Professor of Public Policy and Corporate Responsibility, Professor of Economics and Finance, Columbia University Graduate School of Business; Director of the Earth Institute Center for Economy, Environment, and Society, Columbia University

Ravi Kanbur, T.H. Lee Professor of World Affairs, International Professor of Applied Economics and Management and Professor of Economics, Cornell University

Alan B. Krueger, Bendheim Professor of Economics and Public Affairs, Princeton University

Nora Lustig, Samuel Z. Stone Professor of Latin American Economics, Tulane University

Jil Matheson, Former United Kingdom National Statistician

Thomas Piketty, Professor, Paris School of Economics

Walter Radermacher, Former Director-General, Eurostat

Chiara Saraceno, Honorary Fellow at the Collegio Carlo Alberto, Turin

Arthur Stone, Senior Behavioral Scientist, Professor of Psychology, University of Southern California

Yang Yao, Director of CCER and Dean of National School of Development, Peking University

Rapporteurs

Marco Mira d'Ercole, OECD

Elizabeth Beasley, CEPREMAP and Sciences-Po

PUBLISHING IN THE PUBLIC INTEREST

Thank you for reading this book published by The New Press. The New Press is a nonprofit, public interest publisher. New Press books and authors play a crucial role in sparking conversations about the key political and social issues of our day.

We hope you enjoyed this book and that you will stay in touch with The New Press. Here are a few ways to stay up to date with our books, events, and the issues we cover:

- Sign up at www.thenewpress.com/subscribe to receive updates on New Press authors and issues and to be notified about local events
- Like us on Facebook: www.facebook.com/newpressbooks
- Follow us on Twitter: www.twitter.com/thenewpress

Please consider buying New Press books for yourself; for friends and family; or to donate to schools, libraries, community centers, prison libraries, and other organizations involved with the issues our authors write about.

The New Press is a 501(c)(3) nonprofit organization. You can also support our work with a tax-deductible gift by visiting www.thenewpress.com/donate.